The Smooth Ride Portfolio

THE

SMOOTH RIDE PORTFOLIO

HOW GREAT INVESTORS PROTECT AND GROW THEIR WEALTH... AND YOU CAN TOO

CLINT SORENSON, CMT, CFA

LIONCREST
PUBLISHING

THE SMOOTH RIDE PORTFOLIO
*How Great Investors Protect and Grow
Their Wealth...and You Can Too*

FIRST EDITION

ISBN 978-1-5445-3350-6 *Hardcover*
      978-1-5445-3349-0 *Paperback*
      978-1-5445-3351-3 *Ebook*

I would like to dedicate this book to my wife, Lauren, and my daughter, Raegan. You all are my inspiration. Thank you for pushing me to be the best version of myself. Words cannot describe how much I love you both.

CONTENTS

Acknowledgments

This book would not have been possible without the hard work and dedication of my amazing team and partners. David Stefanick, Max Rockwell, Luke Vernon, and Carter Wiles have worked especially hard developing, organizing, and implementing the concepts in this book to serve our wonderful clients.

I would also like to thank my scribe, Madison Fitzpatrick, for her dedication and guidance. This book is a reality because of your talent in helping turn thoughts and concepts into relatable words on a page.

Introduction

In 2008, I was just starting my career as an analyst at a bank.

Unless you were born in this century, you probably already know what happens next.

Most of the bank employees, especially the financial advisors and executives, owned shares in the bank. Some had huge amounts of their retirement savings in those shares. Why not? The bank had been growing steadily, and they believed in its underlying integrity. What could be a more trustworthy investment than the company you know best?

What they hadn't invested in the bank's own stocks, they invested in the market, and they advised their clients to do the same. That was their job, after all, and many of them had been doing it successfully for decades. Their clients trusted them to take care of their money. Everyone, financial advisors and their clients alike, believed their money was safe.

In reality, they were living the life of a Thanksgiving turkey: grow, grow, grow, and then...well, you know.

They had been lulled to sleep, and 2008 was the rudest possible awakening. Out of nowhere, the bank's stock price went from $57 per share to $5. Preferred shares, which are supposed to be more stable, fell just like the common shares. People thought their investment portfolios were diversified, but everything went down together. A lot of people saw more than half their savings wiped out in a day.

I'll never forget my boss's face when I walked into his office on September 29th, the day of the crash. He had a chest-high bookshelf in front of a window, and he was just standing in front of it with his arms resting on the top, staring out the window, traumatized. He was the senior wealth manager, and he had just lost his personal wealth and his clients' money all at once. I had come in to ask him what to do about the panicked and distraught clients who had been calling nonstop, but he had no answers. He was just as devastated as they were.

Wall Street calls massive drops in the stock market "anomalies," but don't be fooled. We've had three of them already in the 21st century, and there are sure to be plenty more in your lifetime. They hurt, and if they hit at the wrong time, they can be catastrophic. I didn't suffer much in 2008 because I didn't have much saved yet, and I had plenty of years ahead of me to recover. But I saw people who had a comfortable retirement have to go back to work—and at the worst time, too, because the job market had tanked along with the stock market.

Even if you have time to recover, negative events like the 2008 crash can knock you way off course in your financial journey. You get scared and don't know what to do, so you might make rash decisions, like bailing out of the market at the worst time, only to buy back in later when prices have risen again. In an effort to cushion yourself, you end up kicking yourself when you're down.

The Wall Street roller coaster is not a fun ride. I've spent my career looking for an alternative: a smoother, faster, more reliable path to financial freedom. What I've found is in this book.

FEAR LEADS YOU ASTRAY

DALBAR is the industry leader in unbiased evaluations of investor performance. Every year, they measure the average equity fund investor's gains and losses against the market as a whole and publish a report on their findings.[1]

I'll save you the trouble of looking up the reports and tell you what's there. It's simple: the average equity fund

_____

1   You can find their reports on their website: www.dalbar.com.

investor consistently underperforms the markets. Their gains fall behind both successful and stable domestic blue-chip stocks, as well as globally diversified index portfolios.

DALBAR says that over the 20 or so years since 2001, the average annualized return for the average equity fund investor is 5.96% against the S&P Index of 7.43%. That's a difference of close to 1.5%, which might sound small, but it's actually a significant shortfall. Compounded year after year, the gap in total gains gets much, much bigger.

Why is this underperformance so persistent? How do people routinely get lower returns than the very same markets they're invested in?

DALBAR has some insights on that question. In a 2021 report, they found that fund investors who remained patient and didn't focus on short-term market gyrations were significantly more successful than those who let their emotions override a long-term strategy.

You probably have at least one thing in common with DALBAR's "average investors": you want to get the most from your money. That means reaching your financial goals on time, ideally without suffering any nauseating drops in your account balance. If you do what the average investor does, chances are you won't do so hot—at least, that's what the statistics say. So, how do you get where you want to go without spending hours and hours tending to your investments, obsessively watching the markets, and keeping on top of the latest trends?

In other words, how do you invest wisely while preserving your sanity?

It's certainly not news that people are emotional beings, and one of the most potent emotions of all is fear. We all experience it—investors are no exception. After all, a lot of blood, sweat, and tears are tied up in our investments. Your future and your family's future can depend on them. No matter how much money you have invested, whether it's a lot or a little, that money represents hard work and the potential for a comfortable future.

So, of course, you're afraid of losing it. No one wants to see their account balance take a dive, and psychological studies have shown that we humans feel the pain of loss twice as intensely as the pleasure of gain. Fear of loss is baked into your DNA, and it can prevent you from taking risks that are necessary to grow your wealth.

The flip side of fear of loss is the fear of missing out (FOMO), which can be just as strong. We're social creatures, and nobody likes to feel left out. Watching others reap massive gains while you stand on the sidelines is painful, and that pain can push you to take bad risks with your money.

So, you've got two kinds of fear that can sink your investment plans. The fear of loss can prevent you from buying into *good* opportunities, and FOMO can make you buy into *bad* ones...and both of these fears are deeply embedded in our human nature. Without a well-designed plan and rock-solid discipline, you'll most likely fall into one of two traps: tinkering too much with your portfolio, or just buying and holding without ever making adjustments.

Unfortunately, neither of those strategies is a reliable way to achieve financial freedom.

THE TRUTH ABOUT FINANCIAL FREEDOM

In this book, financial freedom is the goal. That doesn't mean some artificial target like $1 million, 10% annual returns, or "beating" the market. It means the passive income from your investments is greater than your expenses. When that happens, you get to stop worrying about money—you're *free*.

No two people have the same expenses, so financial freedom is a very personal thing. No one else can tell you what your goal should be. Only you know what amount of money is enough for you to live your dream life. I can't tell you that number, but I can show you how to reach it as quickly and painlessly as possible.

You see, the number one thing standing in your way is your own behavior.

Most people will create problems in their portfolio when they see changes in the market and then abandon their strategy. They start out with a reasonable plan, but when the market starts going up, they can't resist trying to catch that wave. So, they buy into hot assets, usually after they've already gotten expensive. Then, when the market goes down, they get scared. Afraid it will drop even further, they rush to get out, often selling at the worst time.

This cycle of constant tinkering—scrapping the plan and reacting to whatever is happening in the market today—undermines the performance of your investment portfolio.

Wall Street investing principles don't help. They're based on modern portfolio theory, a set of mathematical models developed in the academic world. These models might be beautiful and elegant, but their fundamental assumptions are hopelessly flawed.

Modern portfolio theory is designed to optimize your expected returns and minimize your risk. Sounds good, right? But it defines risk as volatility—in other words, how much your returns vary from some historical average. That's not the kind of risk that matters. Like I said, the goal is to achieve financial freedom, not to "beat the market." The risk you really care about is the chance that you'll fail to reach your financial goals. Wall Street professionals don't understand this basic truth.

These models Wall Street is so fond of have another fatal flaw: they don't account for human behavior.

Sure, if you follow their models exactly, you're likely to

do well...but a mathematically optimal portfolio is com-pletely useless if you don't stick to it. And let me tell you, in my experience, no one follows these kinds of strategies. They're too abstract. Most people don't understand them, and more importantly, these strategies don't address the two fears that will lead you astray.

You don't need a mathematically optimal portfolio—you need a *behaviorally* optimal one. You want an investing strategy that takes into account your fears and your hopes, your dreams and your worries. You want one that you will faithfully follow no matter what the market is doing.

Remember, your emotions—especially fear—can get in your way. But with a portfolio designed to help you stay calm and confident, you'll reach your financial goals faster and with far less stress than with any other approach.

Some people want excitement from their investments. They love the roller coaster thrill of riding the ups and downs of the market. If you crave that uncertainty, this book is not for you. I'm offering the complete opposite of that approach. Behaviorally optimal portfolios are boring—but in a good way. The approach I teach in this book will cut out all of the big drops. It will ease your fears because when the gut-wrenching drops are elim-inated, you can keep a clear head and stick to your plan.

Sticking to a good plan is the best way to achieve financial freedom.

DIVERSIFY YOUR SYSTEMS

When most people talk about diversifying their investments, they usually mean something like adding different kinds of assets to their portfolio. A portfolio with a hundred different stocks is more diversified than having just one. A portfolio with stocks, bonds, and commodities is more diversified than one with just stocks.

This kind of diversification is essential, but it's not enough.

In addition to diversifying your assets, you need to diversify your *strategies*. By strategies, I mean the rules you follow for making investment decisions. This is a far more resilient and useful way to think about diversification.

Here's why: different investment strategies work well at different times. This seems obvious, but it's amazing how many investors and finance professionals don't grasp this simple concept.

I'll give you just one example of why strategy diversification is so important. Some people did quite well in the wake of the 2008 collapse of the market. Was it because they had diversified their portfolio by adding stocks and bonds they did not have before?

No. It was because they tailored their strategies to what they could see happening in the market. They knew the market was overpriced simply by observing it. They adjusted their investment strategies accordingly and avoided the downside that comes with blindly diversifying into mutual funds and other investment tools.

The folks who did well did not take random stabs at the market. They executed solid, resilient strategies that gave them clear rules for what to do in any situation. When you have clear rules to follow, your emotions have less power to lead you astray.

That's what the Smooth Ride Portfolio is: a simple set of rules to guide your investment decisions at all times. It combines three different investing strategies taken from three of the greatest investors of all time: Warren Buffett, Ray Dalio, and Jerry Parker. Each of the three strategies can be successful on its own, but the real magic happens when you combine them. In this book, you'll learn the principles behind each strategy, how they work together, and exactly how to implement them in your portfolio.

THE MAGIC OF A SMOOTH RIDE

I've been developing this system for the past two decades and testing it with financial advisors and their clients all over the country, and the difference it makes is astounding. It turns the roller coaster of investing into a much gentler, more predictable experience, both emotionally and financially. It doesn't completely eliminate every bump in the road or guarantee that you'll always be on an upward trajectory—nothing can do that (and you shouldn't trust anyone who promises it). What it does is cut out the big losses, which helps you stay in the game long enough to capture the big wins...and sleep soundly while you wait.

Learning three investment strategies instead of just one might sound a little overwhelming, but I want to emphasize that these are completely within any investor's capabilities. You don't have to be an experienced investor or have a lot of money. Everything I'm going to teach you can be done with information and investment products that are available to anyone.

The first benefit of the Smooth Ride Portfolio is that it protects your assets while allowing them to grow. To paraphrase Warren Buffett, rule #1 is don't lose money. Rule #2: don't forget the first rule.

This system honors that philosophy, but not by squirreling your money away in low-risk, low-return assets. You can't grow wealth that way. Instead, it uses smart asset allocation strategies to keep your money in high-growth assets at the right time and move it into safer assets when the risks get too big. That's how you get a smooth ride and harness the power of compounding to grow your wealth.

The second benefit is that implementation of this system is unbelievably easy. Once you set up your portfolio, you'll adjust your allocations once a year at the most. That's right—no obsessive market watching, and no stressing over the daily dips and the rises.

That annual adjustment will take you less than an hour

each time. Think of it: just one hour a year, and you won't be plagued by worries or anxiety for the rest of the year because you know the system will be working for you in any market. You will not have to follow the market or be constantly tinkering with your portfolio.

The third—and most underappreciated—benefit of this system is that it will free you from fear. No anxiety over whether your portfolio is keeping up with the market. No wondering if you should jump on that hot stock everyone is talking about. No worrying about what the latest economic news means for your investments.

The fact is, most of the information coming out of the financial world has no bearing on ordinary investors. Every day you can read a news release about the job market, or what the stock market is doing, or how much value a well-known stock has lost, or any number of other things. If you let yourself, it's easy to fall prey to the warnings and alarmist messages that often accompany these reports.

That's why I'm dedicating a whole chapter to explaining the inner workings of each strategy in the Smooth Ride Portfolio. If I just gave you the how-to without the theory behind it all, you wouldn't get the peace of mind that comes with understanding *why* your plan is a good one. In fact, you probably wouldn't stick with the plan at all, and that defeats the whole purpose of this book.

Once you understand the three strategies of the Smooth

Ride Portfolio, you'll look at the world differently. You'll understand you don't need to predict the market. All you need to do is observe, orient, decide, and act.

That mindset change is what I see over and over among the financial advisors who hire me as a consultant. It might surprise you to learn that most financial advisors don't have deep expertise in building investment portfolios—they just know a little more than your average person. Worse, they might be steeped in outdated methods and theories of investment. Most think that all they need to know to build a client's portfolio is their age, risk tolerance, and bank account balance.

That's not nearly enough. Age actually has surprisingly little to do with it, and there are lots of things that matter more. For example, what's their personal history? What's their experience with investing? Where did they get their money? What's their employment status? Most advisors don't ask these questions, so they can't build portfolios that truly serve their clients' needs.

Plus, they massively underestimate the importance of their roles as emotional coaches. Most advisors care about their clients and are motivated to help them reach their financial goals, but that's not enough. They need to have the strength to stay cool when an emotional client calls them worried that the sky is falling down and their retirement nest egg is about to vanish. That's when the client needs their financial advisor to be a behavioral coach to help them through difficult times.

That's why advisors hire me and my company, Wealth-Shield, to help them build great portfolios and become outstanding coaches for their clients. What I'm teaching you in this book is exactly what I teach them. In fact, you'll probably have an easier time learning it than they do because you don't have anything to unlearn!

THIS COULD PROTECT YOUR FAMILY FINANCES

The desire to avoid financial devastation is what got me into this field. I was in college when the dotcom crash of 2001 hit, and my family went through a dark financial time: my father lost his job, and we almost lost our house. I was stunned. I had grown up in an upper-middle-class family, and suddenly life became hard. To top it off, I knew nothing about finance. No one ever taught me. I was completely financially illiterate.

My grandmother gave me a copy of *The Millionaire Next Door,* which showed me my financial IQ was truly in the dirt. That realization kicked me into gear. Next I read *Rich Dad, Poor Dad*, and soon you couldn't stop me. I probably read something like 40 books on finance and investing that first year.

I was a science major in college, so the scientific method—forming a hypothesis and testing the hypothesis with experiments—got thoroughly ingrained in me. It's a good way to find out if what you are doing really works. I took that approach and applied it to investing. My new goal was to be a full-time investor and, most importantly, to never let something like the dotcom crash happen to me or my family ever again.

So, after college I interned at a big insurance and financial management company. Then, I worked for a bank (the one you read about at the beginning of this chapter), which gave me deeper insights into the vast world of finance. My boss was an advisor who worked with all kinds of investors, from corporate players with lots of money to individual investors with more modest means, so I learned about a wide variety of investment tools and approaches. When the 2008 crash came, I had an inside view of the destruction it caused to everyone—retail investors, financial advisors, and entire institutions.

That's when I began applying the scientific method to investing, and the Smooth Ride Portfolio started taking shape. In 2014, it became the foundation for my own business. I started by helping one financial advisor build up a strong portfolio for his clients, and by 2016, I was doing the same thing for advisors across the country.

I've been serving advisors ever since. This book is my attempt to take all the knowledge I've accumulated through theory and practice and share it directly with the people who need it most—regular investors like you. It will guide you the same way I guide professional financial advisors each and every day.

START YOUR SMOOTH RIDE

You do not—I repeat, you do *not*—need a lot of money to start investing. That said, there are a few things you should do to make sure you're ready.

First, save a cash cushion of about 6–12 months of expenses. If you have an expensive emergency or suddenly lose your income, you need to have some money at hand in a standard, boring old savings account to keep you afloat. You do not want to be reaching into your investment portfolio in that situation. First of all, you might face penalties or taxes for withdrawing from your investment accounts, depending on what kind they are. More importantly, that kind of tinkering is exactly what we're trying to avoid.

Second, if you have high-interest debt, like credit card debt, it's probably a good idea to pay that off first. It hardly makes sense to earn 10% on your investments in a year when you could have used that money to pay off loans that are costing you 15% or 20% a year. Plug the drain before you try to fill the tub.

Third, if you have an employer with a 401k matching program, max that out. For example, let's say they'll match whatever you put into your 401k account up to 6% of your salary. Make sure you save that 6% so you can get as much of that free money as possible. You can even implement some of what you'll learn in this book inside that account, depending on the investment options your employer's 401k provider offers.

Finally, I highly recommend that you hire a good financial planner. Although you absolutely can do everything in this book on your own, it's immensely beneficial to have a coach who can help keep you on track.

Let's be clear: a financial planner is not the same as a financial advisor. Financial advisors typically direct your investments for you and get paid a small percentage of the total amount of money they manage, typically around 1%. Financial planners are paid by the hour and don't manage your money for you—they just help you stay on track with your journey to your financial goal. They are there, essentially, to have your back, coach you, and help you along.

Everyone needs a coach. Even great athletes, talented and driven as they are, need a coach to help them excel. Even I, with all my knowledge of investing, have a financial planner—I need a coach too.

The most important thing to take away from this introduction, and this whole book, is the importance of discipline. Commit to a system of investing, and don't stray from it. Stick to the plan. Don't let market fluctuations or your own emotions lead you off course.

In the next chapter, we'll start by explaining some essential concepts and debunking some myths about money and investing. Even if you're an experienced investor, don't skip this chapter. It may reveal something you didn't know or make you think about investing differently. Most importantly, it lays the philosophical foundation for everything else you'll learn in this book.

Chapter 2 focuses on the first of the three Smooth Ride Portfolio strategies: value investing. In this approach, Warren Buffett is our guide. You'll learn what value investing is, why it works, what makes it challenging, and the role it plays in our three-part system. Chapter 3 is a deep dive into the second strategy: business cycle investing, the preferred strategy of Ray Dalio. Chapter 4 teaches the third and final strategy: trend following, the approach used by Jerry Parker and the legendary Turtle Traders. If none of those names are familiar to you, don't worry. In each chapter, I'll tell the story of these people and show why they are reliable guides to follow in your wealth-building journey.

Finally, in Chapter 5, we'll dive into the practicalities of implementing the Smooth Ride Portfolio. There are a few different ways to do it depending on your circumstances, so I'll walk through each one in detail and help you decide which is right for you. Once you do, the initial setup of your portfolio will take a few hours at most, and maintaining it is even easier.

In truth, reading this book takes longer than implementing what you'll learn from it. You might be tempted to skip to the end and just follow the instructions, but don't. Without a deep understanding of what you're doing and why, the strategy won't work.

So, get curious! If you aren't already, now is the time to become a student of investing. Turn the page and let's get started.

Chapter 1

PRINCIPLES OF A SMOOTH RIDE

You don't have to be deep into the investing world to pick up on some common financial "wisdom" floating around. How many of these nuggets have you encountered?

- The stock market always goes up in the long run.
- Put your money in a target date fund and forget about it.
- You should start investing as early in your life as possible.
- Don't invest in just one thing. It's important to diversify.
- As you get older, your portfolio should be less risky.

Which of these is true? Some are good advice, and others are myths. Do you know the difference?

Common wisdom is tricky—just because everyone

says something doesn't make it true. To be a truly Hy informed and confident investor, you've got to understand the reasoning behind the advice you hear and the decisions you make. Otherwise, you very well might find yourself following the crowd down a dead-end street.

So, before I get into the three strategies of the Smooth Ride Portfolio, I'm going to bust some myths about investing and clarify some basic concepts that will give you the knowledge you need to truly understand how to make investing work for you. Even if you're a more experienced investor, some of what you find here might contradict what you thought you knew, so I strongly encourage you not to skip this chapter. These principles are the foundational reasoning behind the Smooth Ride Portfolio, and the better you understand them, the more likely you are to stick to the plan and reach your financial goals.

THE WONDER OF COMPOUNDING

One of the most celebrated intellectuals in history, Albert Einstein, once said, "Compound interest is the eighth wonder of the world. He who understands it earns it, and he who doesn't pays it."

Compounding is not nearly as complicated as general relativity. Put simply, it is the act of reinvesting the returns you earn on your investments instead of taking them out and spending them. That way, every dollar you earn through investing automatically becomes a dollar that goes to work for you. If you do this, your wealth doesn't just grow—it grows at an increasing rate every year.

For example, let's imagine you have a constant rate of return of 7.2% per year. That means your money will double every ten years. If you start with $1,000, in a decade you'll have $2,000, and in another decade you'll have $4,000. After 30 years, you'll have $8,000. The growth rate of your wealth just keeps increasing.

You can calculate this for any rate of return using the Rule of 72: divide 72 by your rate, and you get the number of years it takes to double your money. In this example, 72 divided by 7.2 is 10, so it takes 10 years to double your money.

In reality, the rate of return on your investments won't be constant. It will vary over time, and the growth rate of your wealth will vary with it. This simplified math is still useful, though, because it illustrates a very important point: the power of time.

Using the same rate of return, let's look at those numbers a slightly different way. Let's say you plan to retire at age 70.

- If you invest $1,000 at age 40, you'll have $8,000 when you retire
- If you start at age 30, you'll have $16,000
- If you start at age 20, you'll have $32,000

The *most important* thing you can do to reach your financial goals is to start early. The longer your money is working for you, the better off you'll be.

Does this mean someone nearing retirement age is out of luck if they haven't started investing yet? No, but it does mean they'll need to save a lot more and achieve higher rates of return than someone who started young. That's hard to do—there's no denying it.

As Warren Buffett put it, "Compound interest is an investor's best friend. It's like rolling a snowball down a hill. If you don't find a way to make money while you sleep, you'll work until you die." Buffett believes in compound interest so much that his biography is titled *Snowball*. Without a doubt, compounding is what makes investing so powerful, and it's the key to reaching your financial goals.

FINANCIAL FREEDOM

As I mentioned at the beginning of this book, financial freedom is when your cash flow from passive investments exceeds your expenses. It's not about having a certain size bank account, and it doesn't matter what you're invested in—it could be real estate, stocks, bonds, commodities, art, cryptocurrency, whatever. If your income from those sources covers your expenses, then you are financially free. Your money is working for you. You are not working for your money.

There are three essential steps to reach that goal.

The first step is saving money. As early as possible, you want to be putting some money away every month. The standard advice here is to live below your means and cut out nonessential expenses, especially if money is tight. That's not bad advice, but it's also not the only way. You can also focus on increasing your income. Uplevel your skills to get a better paying job or take on a side hustle—there has never been a better time to do it. In today's gig economy, there are all kinds of opportunities to make extra cash, whether it be hiring out as an Uber driver or delivering for Instacart or renting an extra room as an Airbnb. If you don't want to limit your lifestyle so you can save, go out there and get more income.

The second step is putting that extra money to work by investing it at a reasonable rate of return. If you just keep it in a savings account or low-interest CD, you'll miss out on the power of compounding, and your money will actually lose value over time because of inflation. Without investing, you would have to save a huge portion of your income every year in order to retire comfortably at a reasonable age.

The third step is making sure you don't lose money. No matter what you invest in, you are going to experience losses sometimes, but it's important to make sure those losses are never very big. The next section explains why.

THE DEVASTATION OF BIG DRAWDOWNS

A drawdown is the difference between the highest level

your account reaches and its subsequent lowest level. In other words, if you look at a graph of your investment account balance, it's the vertical distance from a peak to the following trough. It can be expressed as a percentage of the value of your investment; for example, a drawdown of 50% means you lost half of your money (ouch). The bigger this difference is, the longer it takes to recover and the bigger your returns have to be to get back to where you started.

PERCENT LOSS DRAWDOWN VS. PERCENT TO RECOVER

% LOSS OF CAPITAL	% OF GAIN REQUIRED TO RECOUP LOSS
10%	11.11%
20%	25%
30%	42.85%
40%	66.66%
50%	100%
60%	150%
70%	233%
80%	400%
90%	900%
100%	broke

This chart illustrates the damage drawdowns can do. For example, say you lose 50% of your investment. You don't need to make 50% to get back to where you were—you need to make 100%, i.e., you must *double* your current portfolio value. At a rate of return of 7.2%, that would take you ten years.

That's a quarter or more of your investing life wasted, and the impact on your total wealth at retirement age could be massive. Remember our previous example of the Rule of 72? If you invested $1,000 at age 20, it turned into $32,000 by age 70. With a ten-year setback in compounding, you only get 40 years of growth instead of 50, which means that by age 70, you would only have $16,000—*half* as much.

Drawdowns are no trivial matter. They can wreck your portfolio, and the bigger the drawdown, the worse the consequences will be. Small drawdowns are inevitable and easily survivable, but once they get bigger than about 30%, they become very problematic, especially because they're usually followed by prolonged periods of low returns.

STOCK MARKET REALITIES

The scary truth is that big drawdowns and low returns are not that rare in the US stock market. If you prefer to be a passive investor, it's tempting to just buy index funds and hold them for decades. After all, the stock market always goes up in the long run, right? Well, historically, yes, but it's not that simple.

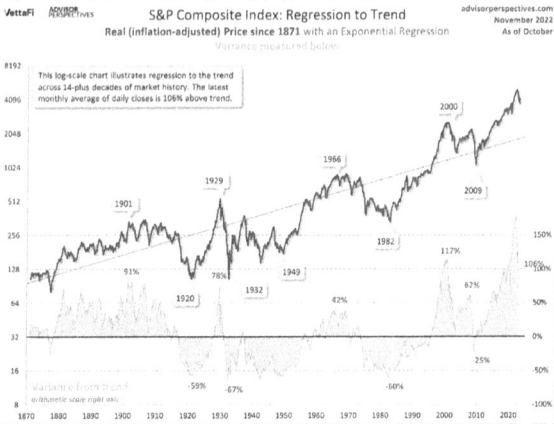

S&P Historical Composite 1871–March 2022 by advisorperspectives.com.

This graph shows why. Over the last 150 years, the S&P has certainly gone up, but it also experienced many large drawdowns and several eras when returns were low for long stretches of time. From 1901 (a high valuation time) to 1920, one dollar grew to only $1.13 in real value. From 1929 (just before the 80% drawdown that sparked the Great Depression) to 1948, a dollar grew to only $1.30. Continuing forward, if you had your money in the market from 1962 to 1981, your dollar invested would have yielded only $1.17. And, most recently, a dollar invested in 2000 took 19 years to become $2.

In fact, if you look closely at the chart, there isn't a single 40-year period that doesn't include some very painful events. If you start investing young and plan to retire in your 60s or 70s, that means you're virtually guaranteed to experience some rough times in the market.

And although the US stock market has historically gone up over the long run, there's no fundamental reason to think that will always be true. A study of stock markets in 39 countries from 1926 to1996 found that the median real appreciation rate was only 1.5% per year.[2] During that same time, the American stock market saw a 5% annual return. The US stock market has been an exception, and it may not always remain so.

Even in good times, not all stocks appreciate. An analysis of US stocks from 1983 to 2006 makes this clear.[3] During that time, 39% of stocks were unprofitable investments, and 18% of stocks lost over 75% of their value. Only a quarter of all stocks accounted for *all* of the market's gains.

Perhaps most importantly, individual stock performance did not follow a normal distribution. A normal distribution is a nice, even bell curve with equal chances of very high or very low performance. The distribution of stock performance isn't so pretty. It has a big fat left tail, which means there's a bigger chance of a devastating loss than a massive win.

---

2   Philippe Jorion and William N. Goetzmann, "A Century of Global Stock Markets" (December 1996), available at SSRN, http://dx.doi.org/10.2139/ssrn.8156.

3   Longboard Asset Management, "The Capitalism Distribution: Observations of Individual Common Stock Returns, 1983–2006," accessed October 18, 2022, https://z822j1x8tde3wuovlgo7ue15-wpengine.netdna-ssl.com/wp-content/uploads/2017/11/The_Capitalism_Distribution_12.12.12_1_.pdf.

Total Lifetime Returns For Individual U.S. Stocks 1983-2006

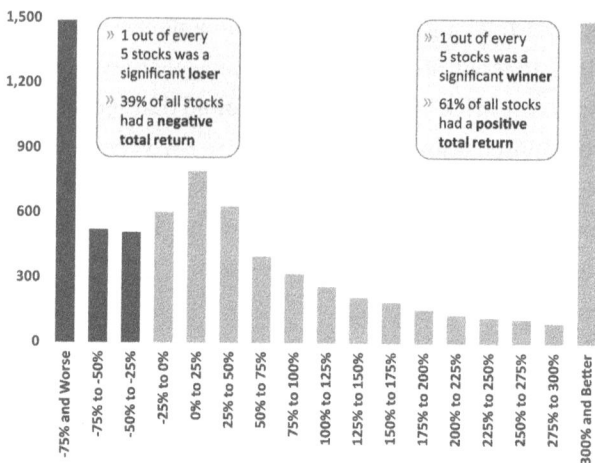

» 1 out of every 5 stocks was a significant **loser**

» 39% of all stocks had a **negative total return**

» 1 out of every 5 stocks was a significant **winner**

» 61% of all stocks had a **positive total return**

Stock Returns, 1983–2006

"The Capitalism Distribution: Observations of Individual Common Stock Returns, 1983–2006" by Longboard Asset Management

That means picking stocks is a dangerous game. One in five stocks is a big winner, but one in five is a big loser, and there's no way to reliably predict which is which. Here's another way to look at it: 64% of stocks underperform. How do you reliably find the 36% that don't? No one really knows, and picking losers can set you back years, even decades.

Lots of people assume the stock market will always go up, and if they stay in it long enough, they'll walk away with 10% annual returns. Reality says otherwise. You are not always going to get average returns, your starting point matters, and drawdowns *really* matter. If you are running around picking stocks, you are at a very real risk of devastating losses.

None of this is to say you shouldn't invest in the stock market or use index funds. In fact, index funds are a core part of the Smooth Ride Portfolio, and they will be the source of most of your returns. What you shouldn't do is simply buy and hold them without ever adjusting or, worse, try to pick individual stocks.

DYNAMIC DIVERSIFICATION

Perhaps your best tool against the negative effects of downturns is diversification. Harry Markowitz, a Nobel Prize–winning economist, says diversification is the only free lunch in investing.

Simply put, diversification means creating a collection of different assets that don't all behave the same way. A portfolio that holds just one stock and never changes isn't diversified at all. If it holds an index fund of the US stock market, it has one layer of diversification—some stocks will go up while others go down. That's not enough, though, because stock prices are still highly correlated to each other. In other words, they tend to behave similarly, which means your whole portfolio could go down together.

To avoid that, you need to diversify by *asset class*. That means your portfolio holds assets other than just US stocks, like bonds, international securities, commodities, real estate, and more. With a diverse collection of assets in your portfolio, you will be better positioned to weather any downturns because some of them will zig while others zag.

A classic "balanced" asset allocation is 60% of your port-folio in US stocks and 40% in US bonds. If you diversified your portfolio in this way from 1993 to now, you would have seen an 8.63% growth with a maximum drawdown of 28%. In that same period, stocks grew at 10% but had a maximum drawdown of 50%. Remember that draw-downs are particularly destructive, so even though the raw rate of return in the balanced portfolio was lower, the risk-adjusted rate of return was higher.

The third layer of diversification is in your investment strategy, as I mentioned at the beginning of this book. The goal of diversification is to hold assets that are not correlated with each other, but correlations change over time. Therefore, your asset allocation needs to be dynamic. That's why the Smooth Ride Portfolio has you adjust your investments every year.

TRADITIONAL AND ALTERNATIVE INVESTMENTS

There's a wide range of investment vehicles out there in the world. The "traditional" ones are available to anyone and can easily be bought and sold online. They include:

- Individual stocks: Shares of ownership in a public company.
- Individual bonds: Loans to a government or company.
- Futures: Bets on future prices of currencies, interest rates, or commodities.
- Exchange Traded Funds (ETFs): Baskets of securi-

ties held in a trust and managed by a fund manager or pegged to an index. The prices on ETFs change constantly during the market trading day.

- Mutual funds: Similar to ETFs in that they are a collection of securities managed by a fund manager. The main difference between ETFs and mutual funds is that a mutual fund is priced only once a day.

"Alternative" investments include everything else: private equity, real estate, commodities, hedge funds, and more. These are the primary vehicles for most of the great investors. Big institutions, like endowments, also allocate a large percentage of their portfolio to alternative investments. For example, in 2019, the Yale endowment had 75% of its assets in alternative investments.

Some of these vehicles, such as hedge funds, are only available to high net worth individuals. That's because they involve securities that are not registered with the SEC, which means they are not regulated like public securities such as public companies and mutual funds. Consequently, they usually involve more risk. Hedge funds sometimes get a bad rap from investors due to their high fees, but they can be a very useful method of diversification because they can do more complex trading involving going short or buying illiquid assets.

To use these riskier vehicles, you generally have to be an accredited investor, a qualified eligible participant, or a qualified purchaser. Accredited investors have an income over $200k in the last two tax years (over $300k if you file jointly with your spouse) or a net worth over $1 million, excluding the value of your primary residence. Qualified eligible participants own at least $2 million in investments and have experience in commodity futures trading. Qualified purchasers own at least $5 million in investments.

The Smooth Ride Portfolio can be implemented with all traditional assets, all alternative, or a mix of both. In Chapter 5, you'll see exactly how this works and decide which path is right for you.

THE FOLLY OF TARGET DATE FUNDS

If you've opened an investment account (especially a 401k), you've probably heard of target date funds. They're mutual funds built around an approximate date of retirement, for example, 2050. As that date approaches, the asset allocation strategy of the fund gets less and less risky—fewer stocks, more bonds—to reduce the chances of experiencing a large drawdown shortly before retirement. It sounds logical, and it's so simple: just pick the right fund for your age, put all your money there, and wait.

In reality, this is a dangerous position to take. The idea that your age is the only important factor for determining your asset allocation is absurd. It ignores a whole slate of relevant personal factors, like:

- Your financial goals

- Your willingness and financial ability to take risk
- Time horizon constraints
- Legal and liquidity constraints
- Tax strategy

Even more importantly, target date funds don't account for asset valuations, the business cycle, and any trends that might be happening in the market. They just treat stocks as risky and bonds as safe, and that's that (even though sometimes that's not true). In short, target date funds are a misguided, oversimplified solution to the problem of saving money for retirement. Steer clear.

THE JOB OF A FINANCIAL ADVISOR

In the Introduction, I said that everyone should work with a financial planner. They will help you plan your financial life, but they don't actually manage your money for you. If you want that, a financial advisor is what you need. You might even already have one.

I work with advisors and planners every day, so I know they're not all created equal. According to *The Essential Advisor* by Jay Hummel and Bill Crager, a good advisor should add value to your portfolio in five ways:

- Financial planning
- Asset allocation
- Investment selection
- Rebalancing
- Tax management

Done well, these factors can add 3% per year to your portfolio, which justifies the fee advisors charge (usually 1%). That 2% net boost is no small thing, especially considering the power of compound interest.

However, this list is missing one big factor: behavioral planning. I believe investor behavior is crucial to the success of any portfolio. I also believe any good portfolio must take into account investor behavior. The Vanguard Group agrees; they once said behavioral planning could add up to 1.5% per year *on its own*.[4] This is huge.

When looking for a financial advisor to work with, I recommend finding one who specializes in behavioral planning. They should be your counselor who helps you plan for life events. Investor behavior, and its detrimental effects on a portfolio, is one of the most crucial factors affecting anyone's road to financial freedom. If they imagine their role is to pick the right stocks, run away. There's probably no such thing as a good stock picker, and in any case, it is too vague a skill to hang your future on.

As you look for an advisor, you'll see there's a plethora of mysterious acronyms behind their names. These are the designations that actually matter:

- CFP (Certified Financial Planner)
- BFA (Behavioral Financial Advisor)

---

4   According to Vanguard's study based on their Alpha framework. "Putting a value on your value: Quantifying Vanguard Advisor's Alpha," Vanguard Research, 2016, https://advisors.vanguard.com/iwe/pdf/IARCQAA.pdf.

- CFA (Chartered Financial Analyst—your CFP should hire one)
- CMT (Chartered Market Technician—your CFP should hire one)
- CAIA (Chartered Alternative Investment Analyst—your CFP should hire one)

Check out the book website (www.smoothrideportfolio.com) for more resources to help you hire the right person.

∗ ∗ ∗

In this chapter, you learned some essential truths about investing. These will come back throughout the rest of the book as I explain why the Smooth Ride Portfolio works the way it does. Here's what to remember:

- Compound interest is what makes your wealth grow faster and faster.
- Start saving early. If money is too tight, dedicate yourself to increasing your income.
- Big drawdowns are devastating. Avoid them at all costs.
- The stock market is unpredictable, and you are almost certain to experience at least one major negative market event in your investing lifetime.
- Diversification is the key to protecting your wealth.
- Target funds are *not* the best way to grow and protect your wealth.

- A financial advisor should be first and foremost a behavioral coach, not a stock picker.

With these fundamentals in mind, let's dive into the three strategies of the Smooth Ride Portfolio.

Chapter 2

———

VALUE INVESTING

In 1941, when Warren Buffett was 11 years old, he bought three shares of City Service Preferred at $38 per share. This was a bold move for a pre-teen to make, especially at a time when investing in the stock market was not a normal practice for most people.

The shares soon dropped to $27, but Buffett didn't panic. He held on until they reached $40. That's when he sold them, gaining a $2 per share profit, which was a huge thrill...until he saw that they kept going up, eventually reaching $200 per share. If he had waited, he could have seen 81 times greater profits than he actually did. This was his very first lesson in patient investing.

From that modest beginning, Buffett became the most famous investor of all time. Using his system of value investing, he has amassed one of the largest fortunes in history, worth many billions of dollars. Unlike the typical billionaire, he still lives in the same modest house he has owned for most of his life. In fact, he has pledged to give more than 99% of his wealth to charity.

For all his success, Buffett is not an enigma.

We sometimes think of exceptionally successful people as possessing special abilities unavailable to ordinary folks. This is not the case with Warren Buffett. He began from relatively humble roots and developed his investing strategy at an early age. Value investing has been his one and only method, and it's not some secret spell or magical mystery. It's available to every investor with the will to use it.

Value investing is ideal for generating long-term returns, and that's exactly the role it plays in the Smooth Ride Portfolio. It won't be the only method we use—it's just the first of our three pillars. In this chapter, you'll learn how it works and what its benefits and drawbacks are. Later, in Chapter 5, I'll show you exactly how to put value investing to work in your portfolio.

THE ORACLE OF OMAHA

To understand how Warren Buffett became so successful and why his track record is so phenomenal, it helps to know a little more about where he came from. Buffett was born in 1930, right at the start of the Great Depression. He was the middle child of three, with two sisters and a demanding mother. His father was a stockbroker and congressman, and Buffett adored his dad and his dad's business. He would spend time with his father at his stock brokerage and absorb the atmosphere and ideas he found there.

According to many of his friends and family members, Buffett showed proficiency at math from a very young age, and he put that genius to work through money. By the age of 13, he earned enough income through delivering newspapers and selling horse racing tip sheets to file his first tax return. In high school, he and a friend bought some used pinball machines and installed them in barber shops and other locations around Washington, DC. He ended up selling that business for $1,200.

At the early age of 16, he had already graduated from high school and enrolled at the University of Pennsylvania to study business. He later transferred to the University of Nebraska and finished his degree at age 19, in 1950. By then, he had accumulated around $10,000 in savings, which is equivalent to over $110,000 today.

A major turning point in his life came soon after college, when he read *Securities Analysis* by Benjamin Graham, a professor at Columbia University. Graham is considered the father of value investing, which is the practice of buying assets whose intrinsic value is greater than their price. Over time, the theory states, the price will rise to reflect that intrinsic value. When it does, the investor sells at a profit. Graham's rule of thumb was to never buy anything priced at more than 75% of its intrinsic value. Buffett was fascinated by this idea and enrolled at Columbia to study under Graham, earning a master's degree in economics.

After graduating, Buffett sold securities for his father's company for several years, then started working as an analyst at Benjamin Graham's company. When Graham retired and closed his partnership in 1956, Buffett took the opportunity to start his own investment partnership with his considerable savings. He committed himself and his company to implementing the value investing practices he had learned from Graham and was always searching for undervalued companies. Over the next several years, he operated multiple partnerships that generated millions of dollars in investment returns.

In 1962, he merged his multiple partnerships into one and took over Berkshire Hathaway (BH), a textile manufacturing company. Within a few years, Buffett had gained control of the company and pivoted from textiles to media companies, insurance, and oil. He used BH to gain multimillion-dollar profits by following a very simple plan. He found companies that were undervalued, bought them, and held onto them for the long run, nurturing them and patiently waiting for their stock price to reflect their full value. Although Buffett has invested in many companies, most of his wealth comes from the massive success of a few who became true giants, like Coca-Cola.

Here's the really amazing thing about Warren Buffett: he was never in the market simply to get rich. As I mentioned earlier, he lives a very modest life. He is one of the wealthiest people in the world, but he lives primarily off his $100,000 salary from Berkshire Hathaway, which hasn't changed in decades. He has promised to give nearly his entire fortune of $100 billion away and has already committed 85% of it to the Bill and Melinda Gates Foundation. He has been vocal about this decision, encouraging other ultra-wealthy people to give away at least half of their wealth in their lifetimes.

Since 1970, Buffett has published an annual letter to shareholders of Berkshire Hathaway, and it has become must-read material for investors around the world. In addition to summarizing the performance of BH and the outlook for the future, these letters often contain enduring nuggets of investing wisdom. For that reason, Buffett is known as the Oracle of Omaha, and financial professionals everywhere pay close attention to what he says.

HOW VALUE INVESTING WORKS

In the investing world, "factors" are quantifiable attributes of a stock that can influence its price. The most common ones used by investors are these seven:

Value: How the stock price compares to the intrinsic value of the company. Undervalued stocks tend to outperform overvalued stocks.

Volatility: How volatile the stock price is. Lower-volatility stocks tend to outperform higher-volatility stocks.

Quality: The strength of the company's financial statements (e.g., earnings growth, returns on capital, debt-to-equity ratio). High-quality stocks tend to outperform low-quality stocks.

Momentum: How fast the stock price is increasing. Faster-growing stocks tend to outperform slower-growing stocks.

Size: Overall size of the company. Smaller companies tend to outperform larger ones (there's more room to grow).

Dividend Yield: How much the company pays out to investors as dividends. High-yield stocks tend to outperform low-yield stocks.

Revenue Growth: How fast the company's revenue is growing. Higher-growth companies tend to outperform lower-growth companies.

Value investors like Warren Buffett home in on just a few of these factors: **value, volatility, quality, and size**. That means they look for companies that are undervalued and have relatively stable stock prices, strong financials, and plenty of room to grow.

Note that revenue growth and momentum are not on this list. So, for example, a high-growth tech company that might be considered a "hot stock" would not be attractive to value investors. Their preferences tend to lead to more traditional (some would say boring) industries, where strong but underappreciated companies can often be found.

Using just these four factors, value investors can adjust to the movements of the business cycle. You'll learn much more about the business cycle in the next chapter, but for now it's enough to know that it has four phases: expansion (when the economy is booming), slowdown (when growth slows down), contraction (when growth stalls or turns negative), and recovery (beginning to grow again).

Value investing works well throughout the business cycle if you adjust the factors you emphasize according to which part of the cycle you're in. Value and quality are always important—you always want to be aiming for undervalued companies with high-quality fundamentals. However, the balance between size and volatility should shift with the business cycle.

In a recovery or expansion, size is more important than volatility. During these phases of the business cycle, companies tend to be growing, and you want to take advantage of that by buying into small companies that are poised for growth. In a slowdown or contraction, focus on volatility. These are the phases when significant losses are most likely, and shifting your portfolio toward more stable companies protects against that.

As I mentioned earlier, Buffett's great genius is in his discipline. With pure value investing, the strategy often appears to be underperforming compared to the rest of the market, especially during boom times. It's during the tough times that this method truly shines because companies with strong intrinsic value and quality tend to hold their value while others fall apart. That's why value investors like Buffett can be so confident that their investments will outperform the market in the long run.

SIMPLIFYING VALUE INVESTING

Value investing, as you now know, focuses on the intrinsic value of a company. At its core, it's about one simple rule: invest in undervalued companies whose intrinsic worth is greater than their current price. The question is, how do you measure a company's intrinsic worth?

It's not easy. In fact, determining intrinsic value is a highly complex and subjective endeavor. Analysts pore through reams of financial data to answer all kinds of questions about the company. What is its return on investment capital? How much debt does it have? How stable is it? What are its gross earnings? What is its ratio of assets to liabilities?

This kind of analysis is way beyond the reach of the average investor, or even the average financial professional. It takes years of education and practice to develop this skill, and analyzing companies one by one is extremely time consuming. The analysts at Berkshire Hathaway do it, of course, but it's their full-time job.

Fortunately, there's another way to implement the value investing system: by looking at the valuation of the market as a whole. Instead of comparing the prices of individual stocks compared to their intrinsic value, you look at the price of an entire asset class relative to the value of the entire economy.

There are multiple ways to calculate this statistic for the US stock market. One is the Buffett Indicator. It's simply the total market capitalization of all US stocks divided by the gross national product. As Buffett said in a 2001 interview with *Fortune* magazine, he believes this is "probably the best single measure of where valuations stand at any given moment."

Let's break this down a bit. If you add up the current prices of all shares in all companies in the market, you get the total market capitalization (often shortened to "market cap"). It's effectively the *current price* of the entire US stock market. The gross national product is the total value of all goods and services produced in the US in a year. It's a rough estimate of the *intrinsic value* of the US stock market because the vast majority of those goods and services are produced by public companies that are traded on the US stock market.

Another valuation indicator is the cyclically adjusted price-to-earnings ratio (CAPE). It's also called the Shiller PE because it was developed by Robert Shiller, a Nobel laureate in economics. Whereas the Buffett Indicator is based on a ratio of stock prices to gross national product, CAPE is a ratio of stock prices (usually an index of the S&P 500) divided by the 10-year average of earnings by those same companies. The idea is that stock prices should be some multiple of profits. When that multiple is large, valuations are high, and when it's small, valuations are low. CAPE is "cyclically adjusted" in that it uses the 10-year average of earnings across the entire stock market, so it smooths out the ups and downs of the business cycle. This ensures that the ratio is truly measuring valuations, not just business cycle fluctuations. I tend to prefer CAPE over other indicators because it's easy to find. Yale publishes the data for free and updates it frequently.[5]

A third common valuation indicator is Tobin's Q ratio, invented by Nicholas Kaldor and popularized by James Tobin, another Nobel laureate in economics. He contributed to the development of portfolio selection theory and used Q to determine whether the stock market was cheap or expensive. Q is the ratio of total market capitalization to the total assets of all stocks—in other words, what it would cost to replace the underlying companies. In theory, the fair market value of this ratio should be one. In practice, it's usually a little lower than one.

All these indicators work the same way: they compare current stock prices to intrinsic value for the whole market, rather than for an individual stock. When these indicators are lower than usual, it means the market as a whole is undervalued, and prices are likely to rise over the next several years. It's the perfect time for a value

---

5   Find the CAPE (a.k.a. Shiller PE) data at http://www.econ.yale. edu/~shiller/data.htm.

investor to buy in. When the indicators are higher than usual, the opposite is true.

WHY MARKET VALUATION WORKS

It may seem far-fetched to think that this simple calculation is anywhere near as effective as analyzing the valuations of individual stocks. To see why it works, you need to understand two fundamental concepts.

This first is mean reversion: over time, valuations will always go back (revert) to average. This makes intuitive sense. If the price of something is lower than what it's really worth, eventually people will realize it, and they'll start to buy more of it. Supply is limited, so as people buy more, it becomes more rare, and the price goes up. The same is true in reverse. In a free market economy, the long-term average price of something accurately reflects its intrinsic value. Historical analysis backs this up.

The second is the power of asset allocation, or how your money is divided among different classes of assets, like stocks and bonds. In studies of investing, researchers have shown that asset allocation accounts for over 90% of the variation in returns across investors' portfolios. So, if you have a diversified portfolio containing many different stocks and bonds, it doesn't matter much which specific stocks are in there. What really matters is how much money you have in stocks *overall* versus bonds or other asset classes.

That's not to say that valuations of individual companies are irrelevant. That last 10% does count for something, but the effort required to optimize it simply isn't worth it for the average investor.

That begs the question: what exactly is a "value" fund? If you have an investment account and have browsed the mutual funds and ETFs you can buy, you might have noticed that some, like the Russell 1000 Value Index, claim to be based on value investing principles. These funds contain companies that are undervalued relative to the rest of the market, according to the analysis of the fund manager.

That might sound like a good way to implement value investing, but beware. Just because a company is *relatively* undervalued doesn't mean its valuation isn't still too high. When the market is overvalued as a whole (as in 2022), even the lowest-valued companies on the market might still have inflated valuations. That's why simply putting your money in a value fund and calling that value investing is a dangerous proposition. That fund is likely to go down with the rest of the market when the valuation bubble bursts.

Practicing value investing isn't about putting your money into "value" funds. It's about adjusting the asset allocation of your portfolio according to market-wide valuation indicators.

VALUE INVESTING IN PRACTICE

What exactly does that mean? It's simple. When stock market valuations are low (according to one of the valuation indicators we discussed earlier), it's a good time to move more money into stocks because prices are likely to rise. When they are high, you want to move your money out of the stock market because prices are likely to fall. (Remember Buffett's cardinal rule: don't lose money.) In those times, it's better to diversify with other asset classes and investing strategies.

How do you know if the indicator is low or high? Compare it to its historical values. If you calculate the value at many points over a long period of time, you get many different numbers. Put those in order from smallest to largest, and you get a distribution.

Let's use the CAPE as an example. If the current value is in the bottom 25% (below a value of about 14), we'll consider it low. If it's in the top 25% (above about 22), we'll consider it high. In the middle 50% (14–22), we'll call it average.

I'll illustrate this with an example. Let's imagine you have a simple, balanced portfolio: 60% in stocks, 40% in bonds. When the CAPE is between 14 and 22, you keep your portfolio the way it is.

If the indicator is above 22, the market is overvalued and a downturn is most likely coming. So, you should reduce your exposure to the market by adjusting your portfolio to 40% stocks and 60% bonds.

On the flip side, when the indicator is below 14, it's a good time to buy more stocks. So, you adjust your portfolio to 80% stocks and 20% bonds.

If you followed this simple strategy from 1900 to 2021, you would have seen a return of about 5.66% per year (see Figure 1). That's slightly better than the balanced portfolio of 60% stocks and 40% bonds, which produced an annual return of 5.08%. It's not quite as high as the S&P 500 Index, but investing in the index comes with much higher risk: a maximum drawdown of 50.8%. Adjusting your portfolio using the principles of value investing reduces your risk dramatically while providing similar returns.

It's worth noting that these statistics are based on annual data. If you do the same tests with monthly or daily data, the differences are even starker. For example, from the daily S&P high in 1929 to its daily low in 1932, the drawdown was over 80% (after adjusting for inflation and dividends). That's a complete wipeout—one you wouldn't have experienced with the value investing strategy.

FIGURE 1: VALUE STRATEGY PERFORMANCE WITH CAPE, 1900-2021

	CAGR	Volatility	Sharpe	Sortino	Max DD
Strategy	5.66%	12.7%	0.29	0.49	-40.9%
60/40	5.08%	12.3%	0.25	0.43	-41.9%
S&P 500	6.64%	19.0%	0.24	0.40	-50.8%

*CAGR is the compound annual growth rate. It's the yearly rate of return that would have been required to grow the portfolio from its starting value to its ending value, if the rate were constant and all the profits were reinvested.

**Maximum drawdown is the largest difference between a high point and the subsequent low point in the portfolio value. The negative sign indicates that it's a loss.

The results are similar regardless of which valuation indicator you use. Figures 2 and 3 illustrate the same test using the Buffett Indicator and Tobin's Q, respectively. (Note that the years included in each test are different because of limitations on data availability.)

FIGURE 2: VALUE STRATEGY PERFORMANCE WITH THE BUFFETT INDICATOR, 1936-2021

	CAGR	Volatility	Sharpe	Sortino	Max DD
Strategy	5.63%	11.8%	0.31	0.52	-36.3%
60/40	4.99%	11.4%	0.26	0.45	-36.3%
S&P 500	6.76%	17.4%	0.27	0.44	-49.7%

FIGURE 3: VALUE STRATEGY PERFORMANCE WITH TOBIN'S Q, 1945-2021

	CAGR	Volatility	Sharpe	Sortino	Max DD
Strategy	5.49%	11.25%	0.31	0.53	-36.3%
60/40	5.32%	11.01%	0.30	0.53	-36.3%
S&P 500	7.21%	16.75%	0.31	0.49	-49.7%

Regardless of which statistic you use, this strategy protects you from the worst drawdowns while allowing you to earn a reasonable return, and it does this slightly better than the traditional balanced portfolio. This is crucial because the biggest danger of drawdowns is that they *hurt*. They make you feel pain, fear, and doubt, which leads you to make poor decisions with your money. Smoothing out the ups and downs keeps you on track to financial freedom.

SIMPLE...BUT NOT EASY

Value investing can be summed up in a saying just about everyone knows: "Buy low, sell high." You've probably heard that even if you knew nothing about investing before reading this book. It makes a lot of sense, but most people can't do it. Why? Because it means constantly going against the herd.

Buying low sounds easy. Who doesn't love a bargain? But in stocks, buying low means buying unpopular assets that everyone else thinks aren't worth much. It takes strength to stand by your conviction that the asset is cheaper than it should be, and the price will eventually go up. That could take years.

Selling high is even harder. As the price of an asset goes up, people get more and more excited about it, often igniting a frenzy of buying precisely when the price is highest. It's hard not to get swept up in that craze, especially as you watch other people get rich off of it. If you already own the asset, there's a strong temptation to hang on and see how high the ride will take you.

So, while value investing may be simple, it's tough to execute. It's designed to get results over the long term—seven years or more. Within that time frame, there will be many moments when it looks like your value investing strategy is a bad idea.

That's why Buffett's true genius is in his discipline. As he says, no investor should swing at every pitch—the key to success is to watch the pitches coming at you and wait for a nice, fat one. It takes guts to do this. Value investors have to have the behavioral fortitude to wait for the opportune moments and the control to keep from swinging at the bad pitches (i.e., investing in overvalued stocks), no matter how tempting they may look.

For example, in the dotcom boom of the late 1990s, Berkshire Hathaway underperformed the stock market, and Buffett took considerable criticism for that. However, when the crash came in 2000, BH did well while others suffered massive losses. The same thing happened again in the housing bubble a few years later. Buffett steered clear of the overvalued stock market and kept massive amounts of money in other assets. When the bubble burst and the financial crisis hit, people abandoned the market in droves, driven by fear.

Buffett did the opposite. Prices had taken a huge dive, which meant many companies were suddenly undervalued—the perfect opportunity to buy into the market. He invested in Goldman Sachs, then on the verge of bankruptcy, as well as General Electric and other major companies that were struggling. He knew that if they survived the crisis, their prices would bounce back. So, he leveraged the money coming in from his insurance businesses to invest at a time when everyone else was reeling from their losses.

Being a value investor is most frustrating in an over-priced market. Those are the times when stocks are getting hyped and it seems like people are making fortunes left and right. You might hear from friends who have made a lot of money in NFTs or crypto or whatever the fad of the moment might be. It makes you wonder why you're sitting there with your conservative, bond-heavy portfolio when everyone else is making a killing in stocks.

That's the FOMO talking. Fear of missing out is a powerful, even physical feeling. A 2004 study showed that social exclusion generates the same brain activity sparked by physical pain.[6] No one wants to be in pain, so the temptation to abandon the value investing strategy can be overwhelming. It makes you want to listen to the people who are saying that the market isn't really overpriced, that this time is different, it's the beginning of a new paradigm.

This happens every time. In 1929, just before the crash, James Fisher, a famous economist, said the market had reached a new permanent plateau. In 2000, pundits said the internet created a new paradigm in the market, and its high valuation was never going to go away. Now, in 2022, you'll find people saying similar things: interest rates are artificially low, so stocks can be more expensive; the Fed's got your back, so we're in a new world of high stock prices.

Don't buy it. History tells us this new paradigm is a fantasy. The market fluctuates constantly. It goes up and it goes down, and that's the true paradigm.

VALUE INVESTING IN THE SMOOTH RIDE PORTFOLIO

In this chapter, you learned about value investing, the favored strategy of Warren Buffett, one of the most successful investors of all time. Here's what to remember:

6   Naomi I. Eisenberger and Matthew D. Lieberman, "Why It Hurts to Be Left Out: The Neurocognifive Overlap Between Physical and Social Pain," in *The Social Outcast: Ostracism, Social Exclusion, Rejection, and Bullying* edited by Kipling D. Williams, Joseph P. Forgas, and William von Hippel (New York: Pyschology Press, Taylor & Francis Group, 2005).

- Buy low, sell high. Buy assets that are intrinsically worth more than their current price, and sell those that are priced too high.
- Don't worry about valuing individual stocks. Focus on the valuation of the market as a whole, as measured by the Buffett Indicator (total market cap / gross national product).
- When this indicator is about average, keep a balanced portfolio of 60% stocks, 40% bonds.
- When it's in the bottom quartile, put more money into stocks (80/20).
- When it's in the top quartile, put more money into bonds (40/60).
- Sticking to a value investing strategy can be painful, especially when valuations are high. The better you understand the strategy, the easier it is to ignore FOMO and stick to your plan.

Still, the reality is that value investing is emotionally challenging. It's highly effective over the long term, so we don't want to ignore it. By itself, though, there's a big risk that you'll deviate from the strategy in search of a quicker payoff. That's why the Smooth Ride Portfolio combines value investing with two other strategies that provide results in the medium and short term. In the next chapter, we'll dive into our medium-term strategy: business cycle investing, the domain of Ray Dalio.

Chapter 3

═══

BUSINESS CYCLE INVESTING

Ray Dalio, like Warren Buffett, is one of the richest people in the world and an investing legend. Unlike Buffett, though, he wasn't a math prodigy. In fact, when he was a kid, he didn't like school much at all.

He struggled with rote memory, which made it difficult for him to learn facts and perform well on tests. However, he did find one thing that helped him compensate for his memorization difficulties: processes. When there were clear and simple rules to follow, knowledge and memory weren't so essential. He could just think through the steps to get to the answer he needed.

Dalio's investing style applies this process-oriented thinking to wealth building, and it has been wildly successful. For more than 26 years, his flagship hedge fund, Pure Alpha, made money in all but three years—and even in those down years, the losses were small. Dalio is now the second richest hedge fund manager in the world, worth over $20 billion.

Whereas Warren Buffett's value investing method focuses on long-term results, Dalio's business cycle method works well over the medium term (two to four years). It follows the business cycle, adjusting to take advantage of growth and buffer against the dips in the market. To understand how it works, let's start with how it came to be.

THE MAKING OF A HEDGE FUND MASTER

Dalio was born in 1949 to a middle-class family on Long Island. His father was a jazz musician, and his mother was a homemaker. By age eight, Dalio was working to earn his own money, delivering newspapers, caddying on the local golf courses, and washing dishes in restaurants. By the time he was 12, he had saved enough money to buy his first stock: Northeast Airlines. He got it for less than five dollars a share, and the investment paid off. He tripled his money, and from then on, he was hooked on the stock market.

Dalio majored in finance at LIU Post, where he finally began to enjoy school. He also began trading commodities, which offered even greater profit possibilities than stocks. This was especially true after President Nixon took the US dollar off the gold standard in August 1971. That decision sparked massive inflation throughout the

1970s, which led to high interest rates and a very tough market for stocks. Investors flocked to commodities in search of more reliable returns.

Dalio was working a summer job as a clerk on the floor of the New York stock exchange when Nixon made this move. It was Dalio's first lesson in the importance of policy decisions in economics, which prompted him to study currency valuation and commodities even more deeply. He began looking at economics in more practical terms, not as some abstract theory but as the interactions between producers, consumers, and other players in the economy, with causes and effects that could be mapped out.

After graduating in 1972, Dalio immediately went to Harvard Business School for an MBA. Harvard's case-based teaching approach, which emphasized process over rote memorization, fit perfectly with Dalio's learning style. After his first year at Harvard, Dalio started a commodities trading firm with a few friends. Although it didn't make much money, it provided valuable experience in commodities, which he continued to trade for other firms after finishing business school.

Then, in 1975, he broke with his employer and started his own wealth advisory firm, Bridgewater Associates. It began with several major clients from Dalio's previous employer and grew quickly, attracting major institutions like McDonald's and Eastman Kodak. Dalio helped his clients' commodities and futures to create price stability in the raw materials they depended on.

Although he had big-name clients, Dalio was still learning, and one of his most important lessons came in 1979, with the downfall of Nelson Bunker Hunt. Hunt was an oil magnate, and throughout the 1970s, he and his brothers had been accumulating silver in an attempt to corner the market. As the price of silver rose from less than $1 per ounce to over $50, Hunt became the richest man in the world. However, it all came crashing down at the end of 1979, when silver prices crashed and Hunt became entangled in lawsuits and congressional inquiries. In the end, he went bankrupt and was banned from commodities trading for life.

This drama showed Dalio the danger of trying to predict the future, as Hunt did. Like most commodities traders, Dalio had always been focused on forecasting, trying to figure out where markets were headed and make the right bets. By the early '80s, he had made enough mistakes to adopt a new mindset, embodied in one of his favorite sayings: "He who lives by the crystal ball is destined to eat ground glass."

For him, trading was no longer about knowing the *future*. It was about knowing how to react appropriately to the information available in the *present*. He didn't need forecasts—the possibilities in the market were far too varied and volatile to rely on such things. He just needed to measure and map the business cycle so he could know how to allocate assets in the right way for the current market conditions.

So, Dalio developed precise rules for identifying import-ant shifts in the economy and the marketplace. He built computerized systems, collected data to model and analyze market movements, and made his investment decisions as systematic as possible. Over time, Bridgewa-ter Associates evolved from a consultancy into the asset management fund we know today, with its famously profitable hedge funds like Pure Alpha and All Weather.

Bridgewater's success was built on Dalio's core philoso-phy of tracking and adjusting for the business cycle. In the rest of this chapter, you'll learn exactly what that means, why it's important, and how to do it in your own portfolio.

THE FOUR PHASES OF THE BUSINESS CYCLE

Even if you don't follow the financial news, you prob-ably have at least a vague sense of what's going on in the economy. People talk, and you can see some things for yourself—business is booming or not, basic goods are affordable or expensive, jobs are plentiful or scarce. Sometimes things are great, and sometimes they're not, usually for a couple of years at a time.

That's the business cycle. It's the up-and-down motion of the overall economy over time, and it has four phases:

1. **Expansion:** You have increasing growth that's above average, a.k.a. boom times.

2. **Slowdown:** Growth is still above average, but now it's decreasing.
3. **Contraction:** This is when you have below average growth that is decreasing. (When growth actually goes negative, i.e., the economy shrinks, it's called a recession.)
4. **Recovery:** Growth is increasing, but still below average.

A complete cycle plays out over anywhere from two to eight years, and in business cycle investing, your money should move around according to which phase of the cycle you're in.

So, how do you know which phase you're in? Well, don't wait for the economists to announce it in the news. By the time they confirm their statistics and make it official, the business cycle may have moved on. For example, in 2001, when the National Bureau of Economic Research (NBER) announced we were in a recession, the recession was already over.

The reason is simple: their definition of a recession is a significant decline in economic activity that's spread across the economy and lasts more than a few months. This definition is completely useless as a guide to investing because it takes far too long to determine if the economy is in a recession or not. By the time the NBER tells you you're in a recession, you've lost any investing advantage based on knowing you're in a recession.

A better gauge of the business cycle comes from leading economic indicator statistics. There are several good ones, including the Economic Cycle Research Institute weekly leading index (WLI), the Conference Board leading economic index (LEI), and my own proprietary index, the WealthShield leading economic indicator.[7] These statistics are comprehensive summaries of many factors, including money supply, bond prices, stock prices, unemployment insurance claims, new business formation, large business failures, real estate loans, and credit spreads. These are all leading indicators, which means that when they change, economic growth tends to follow soon after.

HOW BUSINESS CYCLE INVESTING WORKS

At the most fundamental level, adjusting your portfolio for the business cycle is simple. The first thing you need to know is what part of the business cycle you're in, or even more simply put, whether economic growth is increasing or decreasing. To find out, choose one of the indicators I mentioned above. Take the current figure and subtract the same figure from one year ago. If the result is positive, economic growth is increasing. If it's negative, growth is decreasing.

Now, remember the investment factors you learned about in the last chapter? The two most important ones in business cycle investing are volatility and momentum.

---

7   See the Business Cycle section of the Appendix for data sources.

Volatility is how much the stock price varies over time, and momentum is how fast the stock price is increasing.

When economic growth is increasing—in other words, you're in an expansion or recovery—that's the time to adopt an aggressive posture and invest in high-momentum assets. These are the stocks whose prices are increasing the fastest. There are several ETFs that track momentum. A simple Google search will point you in the right direction. The idea here is that when the economy is growing and likely to continue growing in the near future, you want to own the assets that are growing the fastest.

In contrast, when economic growth is decreasing—you're in a slowdown or contraction—you're going to pivot to a defensive posture by moving to low-volatility assets. These are the times when big losses are most likely, so you want your money in the assets that have the most stable prices. This reduces your chances of taking a hard hit. There are several low volatiity and/or minimum volatility ETFs available. It typically includes companies like P&G, Hershey, Pepsi, Verizon, utilities, and other consumer staples. These companies all tend to trade at lower valuations and have higher quality balance sheets, which makes them more resilient in tough times.

Why not just keep your assets safe in low-volatility stocks all the time? Well, then you would miss out on the big profit opportunities high-momentum stocks have to offer. On the flip side, if you stay in high-momentum stocks all the time, you run a much bigger risk of a major drawdown during difficult economic periods. Switching between these two asset classes according to the business cycle allows you to reap big gains in the good times and protect your wealth in the bad times.

The hypothetical investor who followed this simple binary action plan from 1968–2021 would have compounded at 8.97% per year, far more than the 5.17% of the balanced portfolio (see Figure 4). Even though the balanced portfolio has 40% bonds and the business cycle strategy has only stocks, they achieve similar maximum drawdowns. That means you get much higher returns than the S&P 500, but with a level of risk that's similar to a balanced portfolio.

FIGURE 4: BUSINESS CYCLE STRATEGY PERFORMANCE, 1968–2021

	CAGR	Volatility	Sharpe	Sortino	Max DD
Strategy	8.97%	14.94%	0.47	0.67	-40.4%
60/40	5.17%	8.37%	0.38	0.53	-37.0%
S&P 500	6.35%	12.65%	0.34	0.42	-51.8%

*CAGR is the compound annual growth rate. It's the yearly rate of return that would have been required to grow the portfolio from its starting value to its ending value, if the rate were constant and all the profits were reinvested.

**Maximum drawdown is the largest difference between a high point and the subsequent low point in the portfolio value. The negative sign indicates that it's a loss.

That's a huge difference in both overall returns and emotional experience. The simplest possible business cycle investing system offers market-like returns with a lot less risk—which is exactly what hedge funds are designed to do. To buy into a hedge fund, you have to make enough money or have enough wealth to be an accredited investor, but not for this. Anyone can do this, regardless of how much or how little you can invest.

Of course, as with everything in this book, business cycle investing can get much more complex than this if you study it deeply. However, remember that asset allocation accounts for the vast majority of investment gains. That's why this two-rule system is effective. It executes the essence of business cycle investing in a way that's easy to understand and apply in just a few minutes, no finance degree necessary.

THE FED AND THE BUSINESS CYCLE

Any discussion of the business cycle would be incomplete without an explanation of the Fed, or the Federal Reserve. That's the central bank of the United States, which sets monetary policies and has a massive impact on the business cycle. To understand how, you first need to understand why it exists in the first place.

The US didn't always have a central bank. In fact, it was a major point of political contention throughout the country's first decades. Some believed it was necessary to prevent inflation and create a stable financial foundation for the federal government, while others believed it would encourage speculation and create financial monopolies. That's why the first two central banks, established in the late 1700s and early 1800s, both failed to amass enough political support to become permanent.

Then, in 1907, the stock market crashed, causing a severe banking panic with widespread runs on banks. The crisis threatened to topple the entire banking system until J.P. Morgan, a banker and titan of industry, stepped in and bailed out the system with his personal wealth. This turn of events created a consensus among lawmakers that the country needed a central bank operated by the federal government.

In 1913, the Federal Reserve Act created the central bank we have today. Its original mission was to stabilize the economy by providing an elastic currency, that is, one whose supply could respond to demand. It created new mechanisms for increasing the money supply or tightening it when necessary.

Through World War I, the Great Depression, and World War II, the Fed tried to do what it could to keep the economy healthy. Especially in the years after WWII, the Fed was instrumental in enacting government policies like the Employment Act of 1946. However, many believed the Fed hadn't done enough, particularly to prevent and then recover from the Great Depression. Over time, political support built up for a more active, aggressive central bank.

This came to fruition in 1978, when President Carter signed the Full Employment and Balanced Growth Act.

It called for the Federal Reserve to strive for full employment, production growth, price stability, and balanced trade. This gave the Fed much more power and a much stronger mandate, which is why it now has a massive influence over the business cycle.

If you pay attention to the financial news or the advice of investing professionals, you'll hear a lot of talk about the Fed. In the world of money, people spend a lot of time trying to predict what the Fed will do and the effect it will have on the economy.

You don't need to do that. To implement business cycle investing, the only information you need is the Leading Ecoomic Indicators. However, I'm going to tell you a little more about what the Fed does and how it impacts the business cycle because having that knowledge will help you worry less, which will help you stick to your plan...which is what this book is all about.

HOW THE FED AFFECTS THE BUSINESS CYCLE

So, what does the Fed actually do? When it comes to fulfilling its mandate to maintain long-term economic growth and low inflation, the Fed has two tools: interest rates and money supply.

The Fed sets the interest at which banks can borrow from each other or from the Fed itself. This, in turn, affects the rates they charge customers like you and me when we need to borrow money for a mortgage or a car loan. When interest rates are low, it creates more borrowing, more economic activity, high profits, and higher securities prices. When they're high, the exact opposite happens.

Money supply is simply the number of dollars in circulation. The Fed can increase supply by simply printing more money and buying up government securities in the open market, which is called quantitative easing. The Fed can also decrease the money supply by selling more government bonds and taking the cash out of circulation. Money supply indirectly influences interest rates because bond prices are inversely related to interest rates. Buying causes bond prices to go up, which makes interest rates go down. Conversely, selling causes bond prices to go down, which pushes interest rates up.

Using these two tools, the Fed will try to counter or soften trends in the business cycle that tend to slow down economic growth or cause inflation to rise. Here's how it typically behaves in different economic scenarios.

Disinflation: Economic growth increasing, inflation decreasing

This is the ideal situation, so the Fed does nothing.

Inflation: Economic growth increasing, inflation increasing

The Fed tightens its policies. It raises interest rates and

reduces the money supply by selling government securities in the open market.

Deflation: Economic growth decreasing, inflation decreasing

The Fed eases its policies. It lowers interest rates and increases the money supply by printing money to buy up government securities in the open market.

Stagflation: Economic growth decreasing, inflation increasing

This is the worst possible situation from the Fed's point of view. If it raises interest rates to reduce inflation, it risks creating a recession. If it tightens the money supply, it risks slowing the economy even more. The decision ultimately comes down to the Fed's leaders and their individual views.

To understand how this looks in practice, let's look at some of the economic crises of the past few decades. As I mentioned earlier, when President Nixon took the US off the gold standard in 1971, it sparked high inflation in a low-growth economy (i.e., stagflation, the Fed's worst nightmare). The Fed doubled interest rates in an attempt to stem inflation. It worked, but it also crushed the economy and sparked a recession.

During the global financial crisis of 2008, the Fed used its emergency lending powers to prevent crucial institutions from failing. It also lowered interest rates from above 5% to 0% and began engaging in quantitative easing for the first time. Those policies continued for nearly a decade, until the economy was well-recovered from the recession.

When the COVID-19 pandemic threatened to spark a recession in 2020, the Fed responded aggressively, in concert with other parts of the federal government. It slashed interest rates to zero again and began quantitative easing again, more than doubling its bond holdings from $4 trillion in early 2020 to over $8 trillion by the end of 2021. That promoted confidence in the financial markets and allowed the economy to recover quickly once the pandemic lockdown ended.

Let me emphasize again that you don't need to *do* anything about any of this. You don't need to pay attention to the Fed at all if you don't want to. Everything you need to know to execute the business cycle investing strategy is contained in the leading economic indicators. But now that you know all this, next time you hear that interest rates are going up or the Fed is tapering its quantitative easing, you won't have to worry about what that means for your portfolio.

BUSINESS CYCLE INVESTING IN THE SMOOTH RIDE PORTFOLIO

So far, you've seen two wildly successful investors, Warren Buffett and Ray Dalio, with two completely different investment strategies.

Warren Buffett, as you learned in the previous chapter, focuses on one thing no matter what's happening in the economy: value. When you put his methods into practice, you only need to look at whether market-wide valuations are high, low, or somewhere in the middle. It doesn't matter what else is happening in the economy. In the long run (seven plus years), this strategy pays off.

In the medium term, though, it can be frustrating, which is why we turn to Dalio's business cycle method. By adjusting part of your portfolio according to the phases of the business cycle, you can reap some rewards that value investing will miss while still protecting your assets from dangerous downturns.

Here's what you learned:

- There are four phases of the business cycle: expansion, slowdown, contraction, and recovery.
- Growth is increasing during recoveries and expansions. It's decreasing during slowdowns and contractions.
- When growth is increasing, you want to invest in high-momentum stocks because those are the most likely to capture the biggest gains during this time.
- When growth is decreasing, you want to invest in low-volatility stocks because those are the least likely to suffer serious losses during this time.
- To know when growth is increasing or decreasing, check one of the leading economic indicators. Compare the statistic today to what it was one year ago.

If it's positive, growth is increasing. If it's negative, growth is decreasing.

Adjusting your investments according to the direction of the economy helps protect you from devastating drawdowns while helping you capture big returns when they're most likely to happen. Changes in the business cycle are often driven by what the Fed says and does, so financial professionals tend to follow the Fed closely. You can do that if it interests you, but in the end, all you need to manage this part of your portfolio is the weekly leading index.

Up next is the final strategy in the Smooth Ride Portfolio (and my personal favorite): trend following.

Chapter 4

Trend Following

Just like Warren Buffett and Ray Dalio, Jerry Parker is one of the most successful investors on the scene today. How he achieved that success is the stuff of Wall Street legend.

Back in the 1980s, Richard Dennis and Bill Eckhardt were both thriving commodities traders, each amassing fortunes from relatively modest beginnings. Dennis had famously turned $5,000 into over $100 million at the Chicago Stock Exchange. Eckhardt had studied mathematics but walked away from a Ph.D. program to pursue commodities trading, with exceptional results.

The two were partners, but their views on trading differed on one important point. Eckhart thought Dennis's wild success came down to an innate gift, a special skill that could not be taught. Dennis disagreed. He thought he could teach any person with reasonable intelligence how to trade successfully using his trend following system.

To settle the debate, they created an experiment. They ran an ad in *The Wall Street Journal* seeking volunteers for a two-week program in which Dennis would teach them the trend following method of investing. Then, he would give them his own money to trade and follow them for five years to see how they fared.

Dennis and Eckhardt were well known and respected, and people wanted to be mentored by them, so they received thousands of applications. The two traders whittled those applications down to 14 participants. Those lucky few won a spot in the program based on their answers to a series of true or false questions designed to reveal how well their views of investing aligned with the methods of trend following. This elite group came to be called the Turtle Traders.

The most successful of all the Turtles is Jerry Parker, now a legend in his own right. At the time he joined the Turtles, Parker was a University of Virginia graduate working in accounting. In 1988, after five years of trading using Dennis's system, he started Chesapeake Capital, the hedge fund he still runs today.

Parker is a true believer in trend following. It is the only system he uses, and he has been outspoken about how well it works and why. It's not because he's a genius (although he might be). It's because the rules work.

Unlike many other traders, who often use trend following but diversify with other investing methods, Parker is a purist. As he puts it, his strategy is "trend following plus nothing, forever."

In the Smooth Ride Portfolio, trend following is your short-term strategy. While value investing performs best over the long term (seven plus years) and business cycle investing over the medium term (two to seven years), trend following is meant for the zero to two year time frame. In this chapter, you'll learn what it is, why it works, and how to use it.

WHAT IS TREND FOLLOWING?

Although the discipline of trend following wasn't fully articulated until about 50 years ago, the fundamental idea can be traced back to David Ricardo, who made a fortune in the London markets in the late 1700s and early 1800s. His philosophy was simple: "Cut short your losses; let your profits run on."

That's trend following in a nutshell. If the market's moving up, be in it. If it's going down, get out. Take losses early and get out quickly so you still have money to get back in when the market starts heading up again.

I think of trend following as similar to surfing. Your goal is to catch a wave and ride it as long as possible. So you wait, watch for the right swell, and jump on it when the time is right. You ride it while you can and bail safely before you crash. Then, you swim back out and do it again. There's a lot of waiting and a lot of bailing out before you get a nice, long ride, and that's okay. It's just how surfing works. You've got to ride a lot of waves to get the perfect one. The key is staying in the water long enough to catch it.

Trend following is the same. There are lots of ups and downs, small gains and small losses that seem to be taking you nowhere. What they're doing is keeping you in the game so that when a big wave comes along, you're there to ride it.

It might seem counterintuitive to buy when the price is rising and sell when the price is falling. Whatever happened to buying low and selling high? The problem is that you don't know what the lowest low or the highest high is until you've already passed it. It's impossible to predict. So, instead of trying to make a forecast, you just wait. When the price goes up for long enough, it's likely that the low point has passed, so you buy before it gets any higher. The same logic applies in the opposite direction.

All you need is a clear set of rules for when to buy and sell, what to buy and sell, and how much to buy and sell. For example, the Turtle Traders' basic rules were to buy a stock when it hit a 40-day high and sell when it hit a 20-day low. They also had strict rules for money management (how much to buy and sell) and risk management (how much to risk on each trade). As with any system, the rules can get more complex, but those are the essentials right there. The key is that the rules are systematic, not subjective. Once the parameters are set, all that's left to do is watch the price change and let the system run.

WHY TREND FOLLOWING WORKS

The magic of trend following comes down to momentum. In physics, momentum means that an object in motion tends to stay in motion. In investing, a price that's moving will keep moving in the same direction, at least for a while. If a stock is going up, it tends to keep going up. If it's going down, it tends to keep going down. According to AQR, a leading hedge fund and asset manager, price momentum is the strongest factor explaining investment performance over time.

This isn't just theory—it works in practice. Studies have shown momentum is very stable over about two years. That means if a stock has been performing well for a year, it will most likely continue to do so for another year. Not a hundred percent of the time, but often enough that you can take advantage of this pattern using trend following principles.

This fact sometimes baffles market analysts. Why would an asset behave this way when there are no obvious market factors influencing it?

In short, herd mentality. People want to get in on a good thing, so when a stock starts to get hot, they pile into the bandwagon, which drives up the price even further. It's basic supply and demand economics. The supply of a stock is static, so when demand goes up, price goes up too. Then, when a few people start to have doubts and abandon ship, the crowd follows, and the price falls.

Herd mentality creates the trend, and the trend is your friend. Yes, sometimes the crowd is wrong. That usually happens at turning points, which are only apparent in hindsight. Most of the time, following the crowd is exactly what you want to do. If the crowd is creating a high-performing asset, who are you to say they are wrong? You don't need to wonder why the market is doing what it is doing—that's a waste of time and energy. Just follow the trend.

In his book *The Ivy Portfolio,* Meb Faber showed how a simple trend following strategy would have performed since 1900. For every month of the last century, he looked at the moving average of the S&P over the previous 10 months. If the current price was above the moving average, he simulated buying into the S&P. If the price was below, he got out and stayed in cash or bonds. The result was performance equal to the S&P but with *half* the risk. In some years, this strategy underperformed the market, but it also eliminated the major drawdowns that devastate investors and are so hard to recover from.

The Journal of Portfolio Management reported similar results in a 2017 article that described one of the most comprehensive tests of trend following ever conducted.

The authors simulated trend following in 67 markets from 1880 to 2016, using three different measures of momentum: 1-month, 3-month, and 12-month rolling averages of price. With each of the three, returns were on par with the market while risk was drastically reduced.

What's even more interesting is that the returns correlated negatively with the US equity and bond markets. In other words, when you use trend following, your returns aren't necessarily correlated with those of the market you're investing in. That's effectively an extra layer of diversification.

In my own test of trend following[8] going all the way back to 1881, the strategy dramatically outperformed the balanced portfolio of 60% stocks and 40% bonds (see Figure 5). Trend following produced an annual return of 9.39%, nearly twice the 5.53% of the balanced portfolio. The maximum drawdown was only 35.0%, compared to a much more painful 50.4% in the balanced portfolio and 76.8% in the S&P 500 Index.

---

8   See the Trend Following section of the Appendix for more on this test.

FIGURE 5: TREND FOLLOWING STRATEGY PERFORMANCE, 1881–2021[9]

	CAGR	Volatility	Sharpe	Sortino	Max DD
Strategy	9.39%	10.18%	0.73	0.96	-35.0%
60/40	5.53%	9.07%	0.39	0.54	-50.4%
S&P 500	7.05%	14.17%	0.36	0.47	-76.8%

*CAGR is the compound annual growth rate. It's the yearly rate of return that would have been required to grow the portfolio from its starting value to its ending value, if the rate were constant and all the profits were reinvested.

**Maximum drawdown is the largest difference between a high point and the subsequent low point in the portfolio value. The negative sign indicates that it's a loss.

If you compare the results here to the other two strategies you've learned, you'll notice that trend following performs the best by far. That's why, of the three systems in this book, trend following is the one you can't do without. I love it so much that I apply the philosophy of trend following to all areas of my life. Don't try to predict the future—just watch what's happening now and respond accordingly. It's a very Zen-like way of thinking.

If you have strong discipline and unshakable faith in the rules, trend following works extremely well all by itself. That said, there's a reason it's not the only investing strategy I recommend: most people can't stick with it.

THE DRAWBACKS OF TREND FOLLOWING

Not all the original Turtle Traders did as well as Jerry Parker. In fact, some asked to leave the experiment

---

9   These tests were done using monthly rather than annual data

before the five years were up because it was just too hard to stick to the system. The rules may be simple, but simple doesn't mean easy.

When you're executing trend following, it feels like you're wrong more than you're right. It goes back to the surfing analogy: you're going to bail out *a lot* before you catch a nice, long wave that takes you all the way to the shore. In other words, you'll do a lot of buying and selling without much profit to show for it. It will seem like you're making bad decisions and wasting your time, especially when you sell an asset only to turn around and buy it again at a higher price a few weeks or months later. That's called the whipsaw effect, and it's a major reason why people abandon their trend following rules.

All these small gains and losses are par for the course with trend following. As I said before, that's supposed to happen—it keeps you in the game long enough to catch a big win. The problem is psychological: the pain of loss is twice as powerful as the pleasure of an equivalent gain. So if you win one and lose one, it *feels* like you lost two. The losses hurt and stick in your mind far more than the wins, which makes you want to give up on the whole thing.

Overcoming this requires a different mindset around failure. Taking a small loss quickly isn't a bad thing—it's the best thing you can do. As the entrepreneurs say, fail fast and fail often. That's how you learn, and it's how you keep yourself from getting taken down by one bad move.

Take Jeff Bezos, for example. He saw a trend in the '90s when the internet was taking off and people were just starting to shop online. He jumped on that trend, starting with books, and has expanded Amazon bit by bit to encompass many other things. Some ideas, like Amazon phone, didn't work so well. Instead of holding on and trying to make them succeed, Bezos abandoned those efforts as soon as it was clear they weren't winners.

This is a tough road for most people to follow. Our egos like to be right, even at the expense of making money. That's what makes people hang onto declining assets, hoping for a sudden turnaround—selling after you've missed the peak feels like admitting defeat.

But trend following isn't about being right or wrong. It's about following the rules. The more automatic you make it, the easier it is. If you have to manually decide when to buy or sell, those emotions and doubts will inevitably creep in. You'll start tweaking or flouting the rules arbitrarily, and that's when you put yourself at risk of major losses.

Trend following is still a hidden gem because most people struggle to execute it faithfully, and it only works if you always follow the rules. That's why I combine it with business cycle investing and value investing. When only a portion of your portfolio is governed by trend following, it's easier to accept the frustrations that come with it and let the system do its work.

TREND FOLLOWING IN THE SMOOTH RIDE PORTFOLIO

What you've just learned is the third and final strategy in the Smooth Ride Portfolio. Trends tend to last just one or two years, so trend following allows you to reap short-term returns while you wait for your business cycle and value strategies to bear fruit.

Here's what you learned:

- Trend following is like surfing. You watch and wait for a wave, jump on at the right time, ride as long as you can, and bail before it crashes.
- You won't get big wins on every wave, and that's okay. The goal is just to stay in the game long enough to catch the occasional massive one.
- It's all about following a simple system of rules very closely: buy into the market when it's rising, sell when it's falling.
- Of all three strategies in the Smooth Ride Portfolio, this is the most essential but also the hardest to stick to because it often feels like it's not working, which is emotionally difficult. That's why I recommend combining it with the other two strategies.

Each of the three strategies can work well on its own, as you can see from the massive success of Warren Buffett, Ray Dalio, and Jerry Parker. However, each strategy also presents behavioral challenges that make it tough to execute well. Combining them makes it easier because when one strategy seems to be going poorly, the others will provide some relief. That makes it less tempting to deviate from the plan.

Now that you've seen each of the three strategies in depth, you're ready to put it all into practice. In the next chapter, you'll see exactly how to do that, whether you're an experienced investor with a high net worth or a novice who is just getting started.

Chapter 5

CREATING YOUR SMOOTH RIDE PORTFOLIO

You're now well-versed in how three of the greatest investors of all time have made their money. Warren Buffett, the "Oracle of Omaha" and founder of Berkshire Hathaway, champions value investing, a classic buy-low-sell-high strategy. Ray Dalio, founder of the most successful hedge fund in history, focuses on business cycle investing, adjusting asset allocations according to the state of the economy. Jerry Parker, founder of Chesapeake Capital and the most successful of the famous Turtle Traders, swears by trend following—buying what's going up and selling what's going down.

As these legendary investors have proven, each of these strategies can work by itself. So, why bother combining them? Why not just pick your favorite and run with it?

Because—to put it in blunt terms—you probably won't succeed that way. Most people don't.

As you've seen in the last three chapters, each method creates emotionally difficult situations that lead investors to tweak or abandon the rules. At different times and in different ways, every one of these three strategies feels like crap. But for them to work, you have to stick to them in the tough times as well as the good times.

That's why we're going to combine them. Each strategy performs differently, so when one seems to be failing, the others will pick up some of the slack. They also operate over different timescales, so while you're waiting for your long-term value investing strategy to bear fruit, you can still see some wins from medium-term business cycle investing and short-term trend following.

This mix of methods eases the pain and makes you less likely to deviate from your plan. As my friend Michael Gayed says, the ability to stick to a process is more important than the process itself. Discipline is the single most important factor in reaching your financial goals, which means you need a system that makes discipline easy. That's what the Smooth Ride Portfolio is designed to do: dramatically soften the scary, stressful ups and downs so you can sleep soundly and let your money work for you.

If you skipped straight to this chapter without reading Chapters 2–4, I'll warn you now: you're doing yourself no favors. Yes, you could follow the instructions in this chapter and implement the system without learning the theory...but understanding the *why* and *how* behind each strategy is a huge part of what helps you stay confident in the plan, especially when things don't seem to be going so great. Give yourself the confidence and peace of mind of knowing you are doing the right thing—go back and read those chapters.

In this chapter, you'll see three different ways to implement the Smooth Ride Portfolio. All of them assume you have moderate risk tolerance and are investing for a long-term goal, like retirement or college savings for your children. You don't need to read all three in detail— just choose the one that best fits your situation.

- **Simple Automated.** This option is the simplest and most effective for most people. Unless you have a high net worth or are hampered by lots of limitations in your investing accounts, this is the one for you.
- **High Net Worth.** If you have enough money to access alternative investment vehicles (like hedge funds), this is a great way to leverage those within the system.
- **Simple Manual.** If your retirement accounts have lots of limitations (for example, you have a 401k with few options), this is the method for you.

For each method, I'll explain exactly which assets to buy, how much money to allocate to each one, and how to adjust your allocations over time. Regardless of which method you choose, it will only take about an hour a year to manage your portfolio.

In addition to the information here, be sure to check out the book website at www.smoothrideportfolio.com. There you'll find the key indicators you need to follow, as well as extra information for those who want to dig deeper into the three strategies.

METHOD 1: SIMPLE AUTOMATED

For most of you, this will be the preferred method of implementing the Smooth Ride Portfolio. It is the easiest to follow because it automates as many decisions as possible.

VALUATIONS

Total allocation: $\frac{1}{3}$ of your investment portfolio

Indicator to watch: CAPE (a.k.a. Shiller PE) ratio for the S&P 500 (cyclically adjusted price-to-earnings ratio)

When to check: Once a year, compare the CAPE to its historical levels

Scenarios:

- Indicator in the top quartile (>22): 40% stocks, 60% bonds
- Indicator in the middle two quartiles (14–22): 60% stocks, 40% bonds
- Indicator in the bottom quartile (<14): 80% stocks, 20% bonds

Note: You won't have to change your allocation here very often. Over the last 50 years, you would only have had to adjust 10 times, and that's if you were checking monthly.

Assets to use:

- Stocks: S&P 500 Index ETF or mutual fund
- Bonds: Treasury bond ETF or mutual fund

One feasible alternative that automates this to an even greater degree is to use an ETF or fund that uses valuation indicators like the CAPE. This eliminates the need to manually adjust this part of your portfolio every year.

BUSINESS CYCLE

Total allocation: ⅓ of your investment portfolio

Indicator to watch: none

Assets to use: ETFs that automatically adjust according to the business cycle. Search for multi-factor or factor-rotation ETFs. There are several in existence, and some are available on my website, smoothrideportfolio.com.

TREND FOLLOWING

Total allocation: ⅓ of your investment portfolio

Indicator to watch: none

Assets to use: Trend following ETFs that do the work for you. Research trend ETFs and you will find several available for you; please go to smoothrideportfolio.com for more information.

WHY USE THIS METHOD

This method also requires the fewest decisions on your part, which means it is easiest to stick to. The more decisions you have to make yourself, the more opportunities you have to deviate from the plan, which, as you know, is how things go wrong. To minimize that risk, let ETFs do the work of executing the strategy. Plus, holding multiple ETFs gives you extra diversification because each ETF follows a slightly different set of rules.

With this method, you have only one decision point. It happens once a year when you rebalance your valuations component. The rest of the time, you just let it ride.

I've also weighted the allocations this way because I have found this balance is behaviorally optimal. Die hard trend followers like Jerry Parker believe that you should have the majority of your money allocated to trend following. I'm not saying this is wrong, but in my experience, it is very tough for most people to follow because trend following tends to involve a lot of emotional whiplash. The $\frac{1}{3}$-$\frac{1}{3}$-$\frac{1}{3}$ allocation provides more emotional stability because most of the money doesn't move around very often. For these reasons, I strongly recommend the method outlined above.

METHOD 2: HIGH NET WORTH

This method is for people who qualify as accredited investors, qualified participants, or qualified purchasers. As I mentioned in Chapter 1, accredited investors have an income over $200k in the last two tax years (over $300k if you file jointly with your spouse) or a net worth over $1 million, excluding the value of your primary residence. Qualified eligible participants own at least $2 million in investments and have experience in commodity futures trading. Qualified purchasers own at least $5 million in investments.

If you meet these criteria, you can work with a financial advisor to access more diverse investment vehicles, like hedge funds, that could perform better than publicly traded ones. The most important step here is to hire the right advisor—someone who sees themselves as a behavioral coach, not a stock picker, and who understands the purpose and value of the Smooth Ride Portfolio.

Then, you'll divide your money equally among the three strategies: ⅓ for value investing, ⅓ for business cycle investing, and ⅓ for trend following. There are hedge funds and other investment vehicles that practice each of these strategies. For example, you could buy stock in Berkshire Hathaway, Warren Buffett's company, which practices value investing. For business cycle investing, Ray Dalio's Bridgewater Pure Alpha is an excellent option. For trend following, Jerry Parker and Bill Eckhart both run hedge funds you could buy into.

By investing in these funds, you essentially automate your entire portfolio. The managers of the funds execute the strategy for you, so you don't have to lift a finger, except perhaps to rebalance your portfolio once a year. Your advisor will help you select appropriate funds, ideally diversifying across several within each strategy (if possible).

Obviously, the drawback of this method is the high buy-in, which is out of reach for most investors. However, if you do have a high net worth, the advantages of this method are that it's fully automated and uses the highest-performing investment vehicles available. Hedge funds' ability to invest in a wider variety of assets tends to help to boost returns and manage risks over the long run. In addition, working with a financial advisor gives you the benefit of active tax management, which helps you keep more of your money. You only need to do one annual review to rebalance your assets.

METHOD 3: SIMPLE MANUAL

This is the least preferred method because it requires more manual decision-making. However, I am including it here for those of you who have your investment money tied up in a 401k with limited options.

VALUATIONS

This is exactly the same as the Valuations Component of Method 1. I'll repeat it here so you don't have to flip back.

Total allocation: ⅓ of your investment portfolio

Indicator to watch: Shiller PE ratio for the S&P 500 (cyclically adjusted price-to-earnings ratio)

When to check: Once a year, check the Shiller PE, compare it to the reference points below, and follow the rules.

Scenarios:

- Indicator in the top quartile (>22): 40% stocks, 60% bonds
- Indicator in the middle two quartiles (14–22): 60% stocks, 40% bonds
- Indicator in the bottom quartile (<14): 80% stocks, 20% bonds

Note: You won't have to change your allocation here very often. Over the last 50 years, you would only have had to adjust 10 times, and that's if you were checking monthly.

Assets to use:

- Stocks: S&P 500 Index ETF or mutual fund
- Bonds: Treasury bond ETF or mutual fund

BUSINESS CYCLE

Total allocation: ⅓ of your investment portfolio

Indicator to watch: ECRI weekly leading index, published at advisorperspective.com. You can also use our proprietary index, which you can find on the book website: www.smoothrideportfolio.com.

When to check: Once a month. Subtract the same indicator from 12 months prior to get the year-over-year change.

Scenarios:

- Change is positive: Move all money to momentum
- Change is negative: Move all money to low volatility

Assets to use:

- Momentum ETF
- Low volatility ETF

TREND FOLLOWING

Total allocation: 1/3 of your investment portfolio

Indicator to watch: broad stock market ETF

When to check: Once a month, compare to the 10-month simple moving average, which you can find on the book website: www.smoothrideportfolio.com.

Scenarios:

- Above the moving average: Move all money to stocks

- Below the moving average: Move all money to bonds

Assets to use:

- Stocks: S&P 500 Index ETF or mutual fund
- Bonds: Treasury bond ETF or mutual fund

WHY USE THIS METHOD

As you can see, this method requires monthly manual checks and decisions. Not only is that more time consuming, but it's also riskier because it creates lots of opportunities to break the rules. That's why I don't recommend it unless it's the only way for you to implement the Smooth Ride Portfolio. Whatever situation you're in, automate as much as you can and only do things manually if you absolutely must.

When you do make those manual decisions, be like a robot. Check the indicators, move the money if you need to, and don't waste any time evaluating the choice or second-guessing your moves. Just do it. That way, it will only take a few minutes a month, and you'll minimize the risk of veering off course.

OVERALL PORTFOLIO PERFORMANCE

All three of these methods are implementations of the Smooth Ride Portfolio. They require a minimum amount of time and effort on your part. They automate investing as much as possible, and they minimize the disconcerting and stress-inducing ups and downs you would have to endure by employing any of these methods in isolation.

To see how well this works, let's look at how Method 3 compares to the S&P 500 and to a balanced portfolio of 60% stocks and 40% bonds, going all the way back to 1881 (see Figure 6). (We're using this method to test because it just uses index funds, which we can model farther back in time than managed ETFs.) As you can see, the Smooth Ride Portfolio would have provided higher returns (7.17% versus 5.53%) with far less risk (maximum drawdown of 38.9% versus 76.8%).

FIGURE 6: SMOOTH RIDE PORTFOLIO PERFORMANCE, 1881–2021

	CAGR	Volatility	Sharpe	Sortino	Max DD
Strategy	7.17%	9.16%	0.56	2.77	-38.9%
60/40	5.12%	14.94%	0.21	1.65	-50.4%
S&P 500	6.66%	12.64%	0.37	1.49	-76.8%

*CAGR is the compound annual growth rate. It's the yearly rate of return that would have been required to grow the portfolio from its starting value to its ending value, if the rate were constant and all the profits were reinvested.

**Maximum drawdown is the largest difference between a high point and the subsequent low point in the portfolio value. The negative sign indicates that it's a loss.

Again, sticking with Method 3, let's look at how a real life example might play out. Let's say the market is riding high and the consensus is that it is overvalued. It looks like the bubble is about to burst. So, in your valuations bucket, you'll be in a defensive position, with 60% of your money in bonds and just 40% in stocks.

When the bubble starts to burst, your trend following indicator will tell you to get out of the market, so you'll move all the money in your trend following bucket from stocks to bonds. The business cycle indicator will also tell you to move your money in that bucket from momentum to low volatility assets. That's two more defensive moves to protect your wealth from the downturn. By this point, you have 55% of your total assets in bonds, 25% in low volatility stocks, and just 20% in the broader stock market.

Then, you wait for the market to go back up. When it does, the rules you have in place will allow you to take advantage. Step by step, you'll put your money back into the market to take advantage of the upturn.

The real beauty of it all is that this is a system of simple, easily automated rules. You don't have to try to guess what the market will do. You don't have to do research to pick individual stocks. Just watch the indicators and do what they tell you. The Smooth Ride Portfolio will put you in the best position to take advantage of—or protect yourself from—the market.

CONCLUSION

Throughout this book, I have emphasized the importance of good planning. Financial freedom depends on it, and any competent investor or financial professional will tell you exactly that.

But, as boxing champ Mike Tyson once said, "Everyone has a plan until they get punched in the mouth." When investors get hit with big losses, the temptation to abandon the plan is strong. Emotions take over, and that's when you're prone to make decisions based on fear—and damage your financial future in the process.

I designed the Smooth Ride Portfolio to keep you from getting punched in the mouth. It protects you from large losses, which is the number one reason people abandon their investing strategies. By eliminating overwhelming losses, you stay in the game. You position yourself to capture gains and keep compounding over the long haul.

You stick to your plan and sleep well at night, knowing you're on track toward your financial goals.

In addition to all those benefits, this approach is easy to implement and easy to maintain. For most people, it will take about less than an hour a year to tend to their portfolio. There's no need to fiddle or tinker—just set it, sit back, and let the power of compounding work for you.

ON THE SHOULDERS OF GIANTS

This investing method did not come from thin air or from my personal experience alone. As you've seen, it's based on the wisdom of some of the greatest investors who have ever lived: Warren Buffett, Ray Dalio, and Jerry Parker. Each of these investing legends has a distinct approach to wealth-building that you can imitate with nothing more than what you learn from this book.

Of course, things can get much more complex than what I've outlined here, but we're taking advantage of the 80/20 principle: 80% of the rewards come from 20% of the efforts. You don't need to become a financial whiz or spend half your life following the markets to do this. You can, if you really want to, and you'll almost certainly reap some extra benefits from the effort...but you have better things to do with your time. It only takes a little knowledge and a few minutes a year to get most of the benefits from these strategies.

Warren Buffett, Ray Dalio, and Jerry Parker were the

icons I used to illustrate the elements of the portfolio, but they are by no means the only investors to have found financial success with these strategies. People around the world study and use value investing, business cycle investing, and trend following every day. When you look at the individual elements of this portfolio, nothing is new.

The magic is in the combination. Each of these three investment strategies will experience losses at times—that's inevitable—but by merging them into one hybrid strategy, you can minimize the size of those downturns and keep them from crippling your financial future.

IT'S ALL ABOUT BEHAVIOR

When I first met Jim, one of the financial advisors I work with, his professional life revolved around responding to his clients' emotional roller coasters. Jim was a young guy who dealt primarily with a younger clientele, mostly first-generation wealth owners who had built and sold lucrative businesses. Many were very aggressive investors. They chased big returns, looking for the major payoff, with little patience for anything less. Their investment decisions were often irrational, as were their emotional responses when things didn't go their way.

To be blunt, their challenging behavior was making Jim miserable. Plus, it was making it hard for him to be an effective advisor. Something had to change.

That's when he started working with me and adopted

the principles of the Smooth Ride Portfolio. He began coaching his clients the same way I've been coaching you in this book: to understand the why and how behind their investing strategies so every little bump in the road doesn't feel like impending doom. To seek to grow their wealth when the opportunities are ripe and protect it when danger is coming. To stop trying to predict the unpredictable and just watch what's happening.

Since then, his business has tripled. His clients realize he has a process that works and they have the confidence to stick with him. When the markets are sluggish, they understand how their investing strategy responds by dialing down risk and volatility and dialing up quality. They see how the trend-following components move them into commodities when inflation starts ramping up. They see all these mechanisms at play, each of them working to keep their portfolio healthy.

Plus, Jim now has his life back because he no longer has to run damage control with emotional clients at all hours. They experience much less turmoil because they see the rationale for every choice in the portfolio. They have stopped focusing on returns and pay more attention to the process, which means they don't abandon their strategy or take ill-advised risks at the wrong time.

The principles of the Smooth Ride Portfolio—the exact same ones you've learned in this book—have made Jim and his clients much happier. I think they will do the same for you.

IT'S OKAY TO START SMALL

Jim's clients are high-net-worth folks, but this method is not only for those people. Any investor can implement it, no matter how much or how little wealth they have.

In fact, your most powerful ally isn't dollars—it's time. The more time you have, the better compounding can work for you. So, start as soon as possible.

Investing is like planting a tree. The best time to do it is 20 years ago. The second best time is now. Start as young as you possibly can. Don't put it off or waste time worrying that it's too late. Just keep building skills to enhance your income and invest that extra income in assets that will yield returns.

In any case, make a plan and stick to it. As I said before, the ability to stick to a plan is even more important than the plan itself. Obviously, the Smooth Ride Portfolio is the plan I recommend to any investor. It will give you the confidence to stick with investing over the long term and not get burned out or punched in the face. It will keep you from second-guessing, becoming overly loss-averse, and abandoning the market.

That said, you might decide the Smooth Ride Portfolio isn't for you, and that's fine. Find a different plan, but don't go without one.

WHAT TO DO NOW

Start investing. Don't wait. Bookmark this page so you can come back to it later and go set up an account with Schwab, Fidelity, Robin Hood, or any of the other options available to you. There are a lot of good ones out there. Do it now.

Learn as much as you can. To be a successful investor, it's important to be curious. Dig deeper into the investment world and acquire knowledge and skills. Like anything else, the more you know, the better off you will be.

We've set up a website with a ton of information and tools for the average investor: www.smoothrideportfolio.com. We have an excellent financial advisor tending to the content. Go take a look at it. You'll find things you might not expect, like a stress testing tool to help you with behavioral issues. And, of course, it's packed with plenty of solid and time-tested information about investing and the investing world, including in-depth white papers on each of the three strategies in the portfolio.

Definitely talk to a financial planner. Find a CPA or a CFP who has experience with personal financial planning. Talk to them about their process. What you are looking for is a behavioral coach, someone who will guide you through the rough times with confidence. And personally, I wouldn't use a financial planner who didn't have the lifestyle I wanted to achieve. Don't just settle for living within a fixed budget—if you want more, go get it.

Build up your cash cushion. You should have six months' worth of expenses saved and readily available. Go get more income if you need to and save the extra.

If you have already started investing, revisit your portfolio. Talk to your money managers and find out their plan. If you have to make adjustments to implement the principles in this book, do it as soon as you can. Don't be afraid to challenge your money managers on their strategy and their philosophy. You should make sure whatever they recommend aligns with what has worked historically. This book gives you lots of guidelines on how to achieve that.

TRUST THE PROCESS

When the market is on an upward trajectory, you might feel like you aren't keeping up. Don't let that throw you off your game. Be patient, because later, when the market is down, you'll probably be doing better than most. No matter what the state of the market, it's important to trust the process.

This can be difficult to do, especially in the face of FOMO and the fear of loss. You might be "wrong" 50% of the time, but that doesn't mean your system is flawed. It does mean that your discipline may be tested by these misses.

That's why I recommend all investors have a coach. Everyone, even the very best, needs a coach. Every top athlete has one for their sport, and even I have one for my finances.

Why? Because we all need feedback from a trusted source. We need someone to bolster our confidence, help us make good decisions, and let us know when we're getting off track. Even with a great plan, there's always a risk that your emotions will get the best of you. That's why you want to automate as many financial decisions as possible and hire a good behavioral coach to make sure fear and ego don't lead you astray.

Remember, investing is not about being right. You are not in a competition to be the one who predicts the rise or fall of a particular asset or market. Focusing on being right might stroke your ego, but it won't lead you to financial freedom.

Investing is about compounding and protecting your wealth. That should be your only goal.

HEADING INTO A ROUGH ECONOMY

As I write this in mid-2022, inflation is at 8% and treasury bonds are only 2.4%. We're looking at negative real rates of return on bonds.

The government has been creating credit and printing money, which has pulled future returns forward. Based on that, we can expect weak growth in the near future.

Stock valuations are the highest they've ever been. This means returns over the next 10 years will likely be close to zero. In this unfavorable environment, it is a big challenge to buy and hold indexes.

The current picture is very similar to the beginning of the period from 1968–1982. At that time, the country endured a lot of internal and external conflict. Returns were very low for over a decade…followed by a huge boom in the '80s and '90s.

In other words, this too shall pass.

That said, don't pin your future on hopes that things will get better soon. Hope is not an investment strategy. The principles and methods I have outlined in this book will protect you as much as possible from this tough economy. Stay disciplined, stay on the path. If you do, you will weather this storm better than most.

I'm not saying it's going to be fun. It will be challenging. You will experience ups and downs. I compare it to exercising. For most of us, lifting heavy weights or running long distances is not exactly a pleasurable sensation in the moment. You're literally tearing muscles to make them grow. That can be painful, but it's how growth happens.

It works in the financial sphere the same way. Painful times lead to growth down the road. Don't ever forget that. Weather the storm to enjoy the calm on the other side.

How we view events is a matter of perspective. Down times don't necessarily have to be seen as negative. Our trio of superstar investors don't see things that way. They assess the situation and make adjustments based on their observations. You should do the same.

The future is incredible. Humanity is going to space, building the multiverse, harnessing new forms of energy, curing diseases, and doing so many more fantastic things—things that will ultimately support plenty of economic activity.

Don't lose sight of that simply because the moment feels difficult. We can all come out of these challenging times closer to financial freedom...if we stick to the plan.

Appendix

In this Appendix, you'll find the complete tests I conducted to demonstrate the hypothetical past performance of the investment strategies described in this book. In addition to the tables that were included in the body of the book (replicated here for convenience), there are graphs depicting performance and drawdowns year by year, starting with the earliest year data was available. The data sources and test procedures are also described here in greater detail. If you have any questions about these tests, please contact me through the book website: www.smoothrideportfolio.com.

Value: Shiller CAPE (Annual)

TEST PROCEDURE

At the end of each year, evaluate the quartile of the Shiller CAPE ratio. If it's in the top quartile, allocate 40% to the S&P 500 and 60% to 10-Year Treasuries the following year. If it's in the second or third quartiles, allocate 60% to the S&P 500 and 40% to 10-Year Treasuries the following year. If it's in the bottom quartile, allocate 80% to the S&P 500 and 20% to 10-Year Treasuries the following year.

DATA SOURCES

- CAPE ratio, S&P 500, and 10-Year Treasury pre-1928 from Shiller data set published by Yale University
- 10-Year Treasury post-1928 data published by NYU Stern School of Business

FIGURE A1: VALUE STRATEGY PERFORMANCE WITH CAPE, 1900-2021

	CAGR	Volatility	Sharpe	Sortino	Max DD
Strategy	5.66%	12.7%	0.29	0.49	-40.9%
60/40	5.08%	12.3%	0.25	0.43	-41.9%
S&P 500	6.64%	19.0%	0.24	0.40	-50.8%

Performance

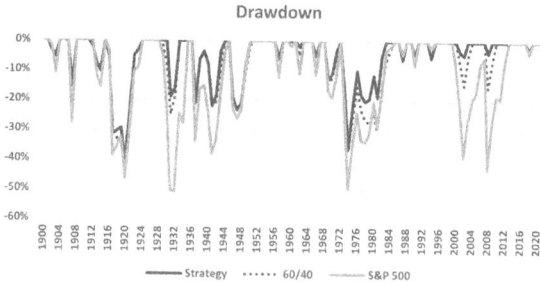

Drawdown

VALUE: BUFFETT INDICATOR

TEST PROCEDURE

At the end of each year, evaluate the quartile of the Market Cap to GDP ratio. If it's in the top quartile, allocate 40% to the S&P 500 and 60% to 10-Year Treasuries the following year. If it's in the second or third quartiles, allocate 60% to the S&P 500 and 40% to 10-Year Treasuries the following year. If it's in the bottom quartile, allocate 80% to the S&P 500 and 20% to 10-Year Treasuries the following year.

DATA SOURCES

- S&P 500 and 10-Year Treasury pre-1928 from Shiller data set published by Yale University
- 10-Year Treasury post-1928 data published by NYU Stern School of Business
- US Market Cap from the following sources:
  - 1936–1975 SEC Annual Report
  - 1975–2020 World Bank Data

- ◦ 2021 Wilshire 5000 Index value as of 12/31/2021
- GDP from Bloomberg ("Nominal US GDP, Annual")

FIGURE A2: VALUE STRATEGY PERFORMANCE WITH THE BUFFETT INDICATOR, 1936–2021

	CAGR	Volatility	Sharpe	Sortino	Max DD
Strategy	5.63%	11.8%	0.31	0.52	-36.3%
60/40	4.99%	11.4%	0.26	0.45	-36.3%
S&P 500	6.76%	17.4%	0.27	0.44	-49.7%

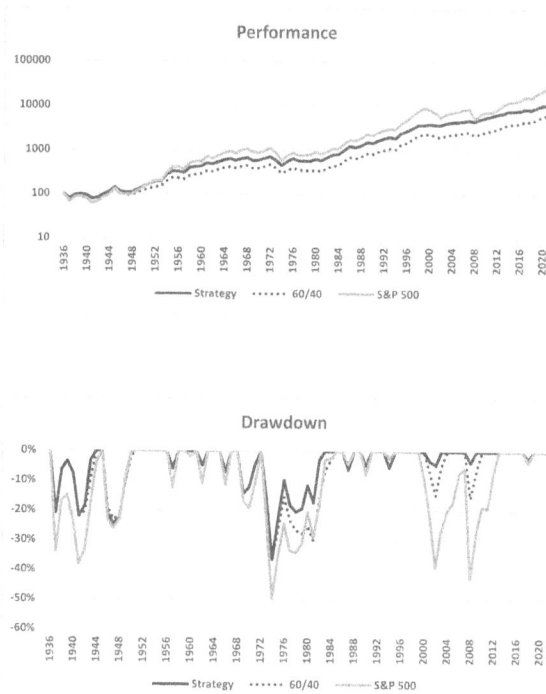

Performance

Drawdown

Value: Tobin's Q

TEST PROCEDURE

At the end of each year, evaluate the quartile of the Tobin's Q ratio. If it's in the top quartile, allocate 40% to the S&P 500 and 60% to 10-Year Treasuries the following year. If it's in the second or third quartiles, allocate 60% to the S&P 500 and 40% to 10-Year Treasuries the following year. If it's in the bottom quartile, allocate 80% to the S&P 500 and 20% to 10-Year Treasuries the following year.

DATA SOURCES

- S&P 500 and 10-Year Treasury pre-1928 from Shiller data set published by Yale University
- 10-Year Treasury post-1928 data published by NYU Stern School of Business
- Tobin's Q ratio is calculated as the "FOF Balance Sheet of Nonfinancial Corp Corporate Equities Liability" divided by "FOF Balance Sheet of Nonfinancial Corp Net Worth Market Value" from Bloomberg

FIGURE A3: VALUE STRATEGY PERFORMANCE WITH TOBIN'S Q, 1945-2021

	CAGR	Volatility	Sharpe	Sortino	Max DD
Strategy	5.49%	11.25%	0.31	0.53	-36.3%
60/40	5.32%	11.01%	0.30	0.53	-36.3%
S&P 500	7.21%	16.75%	0.31	0.49	-49.7%

Performance

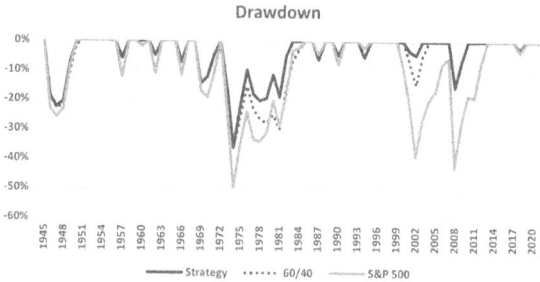

Drawdown

Business Cycle

TEST PROCEDURE

Evaluate the year-over-year change in the ECRI Weekly Leading Index level at the end of each month. If positive then allocate to momentum, if negative then allocate to low volatility for the next month.

DATA SOURCES

- ECRI Weekly Leading Index from Economic Cycle Research Institute
- Low Volatility
  - Before 3/31/1972: Fama French data set, lowest decile by 60-day trailing variance
  - Starting 3/31/1972: S&P 500 Low Volatility Total Return Index
- Momentum
  - Before 1/31/1975: Fama French data set
  - Starting 1/31/1975: MSCI USA Momentum Total Return Index
- Returns adjusted for inflation using CPI from Shiller data set published by Yale University

FIGURE A4: BUSINESS CYCLE STRATEGY PERFORMANCE, 1968–2021

	CAGR	Volatility	Sharpe	Sortino	Max DD
Strategy	8.97%	14.94%	0.47	0.67	-40.4%
60/40	5.17%	8.37%	0.38	0.53	-37.0%
S&P 500	6.35%	12.65%	0.34	0.42	-51.8%

Performance

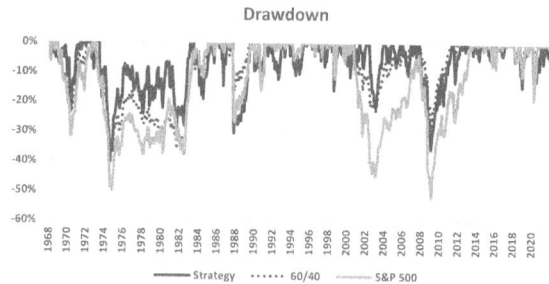

Drawdown

TREND FOLLOWING

TEST PROCEDURE

At the end of each month, compare the S&P 500 price (nominal) to its 10-month simple moving average. If the price is above the moving average, allocate to the S&P 500 Total Real Return Index for the next month. If below, allocate to 10-Year Treasuries.

DATA SOURCES

- S&P 500 and 10-Year Treasury pre-1928 from Shiller data set published by Yale University
- 10-Year Treasury post-1928 data published by NYU Stern School of Business

FIGURE A5: TREND FOLLOWING STRATEGY PERFORMANCE, 1881–2021[10]

	CAGR	Volatility	Sharpe	Sortino	Max DD
Strategy	9.39%	10.18%	0.73	0.96	-35.0%
60/40	5.53%	9.07%	0.39	0.54	-50.4%
S&P 500	7.05%	14.17%	0.36	0.47	-76.8%

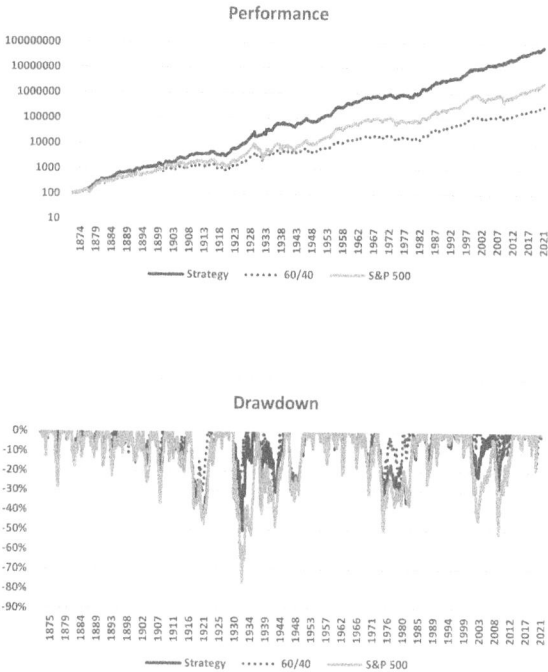

Performance

Drawdown

---

10   These tests were done using monthly rather than annual data

Total Portfolio

TEST PROCEDURE

1/3 allocated to the Trend Following strategy, 1/3 allocated to the Business Cycle strategy, and 1/3 allocated to a version of the Shiller CAPE Valuation strategy that is rotated monthly instead of annually. Because the data for the Business Cycle strategy is unavailable prior to 1968, the portfolio in this test is 1/2 Trend Following and 1/2 Valuation prior to that date. Returns adjusted for inflation using CPI.

DATA SOURCES

- CAPE ratio, CPI, S&P 500, and 10-Year Treasury pre-1928 from Shiller data set published by Yale University
- 10-Year Treasury post-1928 data published by NYU Stern School of Business
- ECRI Weekly Leading Index from Economic Cycle Research Institute
- Low Volatility
  - Before 3/31/1972: Fama French data set, lowest decile by 60-day trailing variance
  - Starting 3/31/1972: S&P 500 Low Volatility Total Return Index

- Momentum
  - Before 1/31/1975: Fama French data set
  - Starting 1/31/1975: MSCI USA Momentum Total Return Index

FIGURE A6: SMOOTH RIDE PORTFOLIO PERFORMANCE, 1881–2021

	CAGR	Volatility	Sharpe	Sortino	Max DD
Strategy	7.17%	9.16%	0.56	2.77	-38.9%
60/40	5.12%	14.94%	0.21	1.65	-50.4%
S&P 500	6.66%	12.64%	0.37	1.49	-76.8%

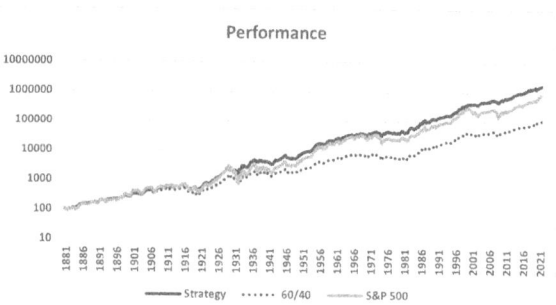

Performance

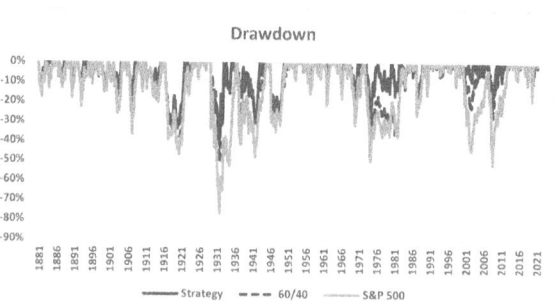

Drawdown